DOROTHEA WOLLIN NULL

# SURVIVING 'UNCLE HITLER'

*Journey of a German Girl*

REVISED & UPDATED

FSP
FIRST STEPS
PUBLISHING

Surviving 'Uncle Hitler'
*Journey of a German Girl*
by Dorothea Wollin Null

Copyright © 2016 by Dorothea Wollin Null
All rights reserved.

Paperback Edition © 2016, 2017
ISBN 10: 1-937333-49-3
ISBN 13: 978-1-937333-49-2

Published by　　First Steps Publishing
　　　　　　　　105 Westwind Street, PO Box 571
　　　　　　　　Gleneden Beach, OR 97388
　　　　　　　　541-961-7641

*All rights reserved. No part of this book may be reproduced or transmitted in any form without written permission from the author, except in the manner of brief quotations embodied in critical articles and reviews. Please respect the author and the law and do not participate in or encourage piracy of copyrighted materials.*

*Every effort has been made to be accurate. The author assumes no responsibility or liability for errors made in this book.*

All photos © Dorothea Wollin Null, used with permission.

Cover, book layout and design by Suzanne Fyhrie Parrott
Formatted for Publication by First Steps Publishing

　　　ISBN - 978-1-937333-55-3 (hbk)
　　　ISBN - 978-1-937333-49-2 (pbk)
　　　ISBN - 978-1-937333-50-8 (epub)

10 9 8 7 6 5 4 3 2

Printed and bound
in the United States of America.

*I dedicate this little book to all "seekers of truth."*

*Our Lord Jesus Christ said, "I am the Way, the Truth and the Life."*

# CONTENTS

ACKNOWLEDGEMENTS ... 6

FOREWORD ... 8

A BRIEF BIOGRAPHY
OF ADOLF HITLER ... 11

PART 1 ...18
1936 - 1943 — BIRTH TO BOMBS

PART 2 ... 36
APRIL 1943 - MAY 1947 — FLIGHT

PHOTOS ... 44-55

PART 3 ... 87
MAY 1947 - OCTOBER 1956 — SURVIVAL

AFTERWORD ... 117

SUGGESTED READING ... 120

# ACKNOWLEDGEMENTS

First of all, I want to thank two people who have helped me tell my story.

Without Merrillin Emery, my former pastor's wife, this book would not have been written. Merrillin transcribed the entirety of my tape recordings and did the subtitling. After my speaking engagements, many people would say to me: "Oh, you must write a book" or "Please write a book," but Merrillin is the only one who added: "and I will help you." How much I appreciate her only the Lord knows.

After we had written the story, my brother, Lothar Wollin, came up with the idea to translate it into German and have it printed in Germany. Without his contributions, that would not have happened. I am also grateful to Ilse, my brother's wife, who assisted him in the translation, and to their son, Andreas, who was influential in getting the story printed in Germany. My niece, Christina Wollin, also helped with translations.

I am thankful for a good husband, two sons, and a daughter, married to fine spouses, and for ten precious grandchildren, most of whom serve the Lord Jesus. What more can anyone ask?

I want to thank our good friend and neighbor Ron Brown, who has patiently helped me with all the computer glitches, and always encouraged me to "hang in there."

Our friend Don Drozdenko deserves my gratitude for formatting all the old photos for use in this project.

May the Lord reward them all!

Dorothea Null
*Florence, Oregon*

*P.S. Since the first printing, my precious sister-in-law Ilse was called home to be with the Lord after a long, courageous battle with cancer. Brother Fred is also waiting on the "other side" for our reunion.*

*All revisions, additions, and improvements in this second edition are due to my daughter Jennifer's urging, encouragement, and hard work. She is determined (after a lot of input from readers and her own convictions) that this little book should more widely be used to help young people grasp the enormity of the devastating effects of war on all people involved, whether foe or friend, young or old. Together with the very talented designer/publisher Suzanne Fyhrie Parrott, they are tackling this new venture. May our Lord give His blessings for all the glory that belongs to Him.*

# FOREWORD

Dear Reader,

You are holding the autobiographical life story of my sister Dorothea, previously translated from English into German and published in Germany by me, her brother Lothar.

It took many years for her to resolve to write down her memories from her childhood until her immigration to the USA in 1956. A few years ago, partially as a result of my encouragement, it finally came to pass: she recorded her story (in English) on tape, which a good friend then transcribed.

When I first received the rough draft and read it thoroughly, I found myself speechless.

Unbelievable things had taken place; horrible things had been suffered by my family: mother Anna (born 1912), son Manfred (born 1935), daughter Dorothea (born 1936), and son Lothar (born 1940). Son Martin was born in 1950, and father Horst Wollin (born 1911) was, for the most part, absent, due to war-related service.

As my recollections from war times are rather sparse, other than a few images that were seared into my memory, a substantial portion of this little book was new to me. I had heard a few stories here and there about events of the past, but we never spoke about this time in depth in our family circles. When my sister left Germany in 1956, I was merely a pubescent sixteen-year-old and had little to no interest in wartime stories.

Consequently, I felt all the more committed to making this draft of my sister's memoir available to as many people as possible: relatives, friends, and loved ones. Of course, no one should feel pressured, and only those who so desired would receive a revised copy. Astonishingly, requests for the book were made, even as it was in the beginning phases of being published.

Many individuals who have lived through inspiring, horrific, and astonishing experiences will say, "I could/should write a book about it." Many never get around to actually writing down their stories, but my sister resolved to follow through and do so. I felt motivated to support this project.

And there was an additional reason I wanted to get involved: as a retired history teacher, I am passionate to see historical data represented with as much accuracy and detail as possible, especially concerning the Nazi era. Because the enormity of the atrocious crimes committed by the Nazi Party—six million murdered Jews, fifty million casualties as a result of the world war that was unleashed under Hitler's command—were so inconceivable, there are some who, even decades after the war, believe that "all Germans" are (were) responsible for this catastrophic tragedy. But they forget, or may be unaware, that the Germans themselves endured unspeakable suffering, misery, and death at the hands of the Nazi regime and their accomplices. My sister's little book could potentially make a small contribution to shed some light on the matter.

Some of what occurred in the postwar times, or within our immediate family, may occasionally seem hard to believe. Does my sister want to accuse anyone? No! Does she want to humiliate certain individuals? No! Does she want those who accompanied her in those times to be put on trial? Absolutely not! And especially not, because she believes that our ultimate Judge is not of this world. If anything remains to be judged or condemned, she releases it completely into the Hands of God.

As this manuscript was being compiled, I would send entire "questionnaires" to the USA; the purpose of which was to ensure that all possible misunderstandings that might occur would be eliminated. Only the most intimate details would be concealed.

Other times I would ask, "Should I eliminate this passage?" to which she would reply verbally or in writing, "No, leave it in there; it is the truth!"

A person who, like myself, is not as grounded in their faith may stand in amazement at the serenity with which my sister

Dorothea is able to accept many things. She went through the stages of being a child in torment during the war to being a rebellious daughter, and then to choosing a life of devotion to Jesus Christ. Even if one does not prefer to explain her calm acceptance in this way, one must respect her steadfastness in her faith, which she found at the "ripe" age of about thirty. I also never asked her to withhold the religious aspects in any part of this manuscript.

Whether or not my sister will go on to tell her story following her move to the USA in 1956 is yet to be determined. Nonetheless, she emphasizes repeatedly, as an overflow of her deep faith—even in the face of many challenging "trials"—that she remains committed to the greatest virtue: THANKFULNESS!

Lothar Wollin
Wunsiedel, March 2014

# A BRIEF BIOGRAPHY OF ADOLF HITLER

*By Lothar Wollin*

Adolf Hitler was born on April 20, 1889, in Braunau am Inn in Austria into a petty-bourgeois milieu. He failed to earn a diploma at the *Realgymnasium* (university track high school) and was not accepted to study at the Vienna Art Academy. Instead, he worked at temporary odd jobs and came under anti-Semitic influence.

In 1914, he volunteered to serve as a soldier, reaching only the rank of private first class. In the midst of the WWI postwar chaos, he founded the NSDAP (National Socialist German Workers Party), becoming its *Führer*. At this point, Hitler had few followers but still dared to attempt a *putsch* (an uprising) in 1923. This failed and instead earned him a five-year prison sentence, of which he served nearly one year.

During the first years of the German democracy, the Weimar Republic (1919-1933), Hitler again had no chance to enter politics, because new economic policies and financial help from the United States, following a devastating inflation that lasted until 1923, brought a new boom to the German economy. Then came the world economic crisis in 1929. Hitler, a skilled demagogue, saw his chance. After several changes of government, he cast himself as "the last hope" for Germany. Many believed his empty promises.

In his book *Mein Kampf*, written during his imprisonment together with his personal secretary, Rudolf Hess, Hitler hinted clearly that he wanted to fight to establish the "Aryan race" by eliminating the Jews and other supposedly "inferior races," and by creating "space for living" by invading Eastern Europe. Hardly anybody in Germany or elsewhere actually read the book, and few who did took it seriously.

On January 30, 1933, Hitler was named *Reichskanzler* (chancellor) by Paul von Hindenburg, president of the German Reich. This unpopular emergency measure was taken only after constant changes in the government, because of horrendous unemployment rates, and after Hitler was able to make his party the strongest in the *Reichstag* (parliament).

Hitler immediately began to dismantle the existing democracy. With Hindenburg's authorization, he used the rumor that the Communists had set fire to the *Reichstag* as a pretext for issuing an executive order, sanctioning the persecution of public enemies. Worse still was the so-called Enabling Act (*Ermächtigungsgesetz*), which in effect was the existing parliament's self-disempowerment. Through lies, threats, promises, and intimidation, Hitler gained almost four-fifths of the votes for this new law. Now he could make his own laws. He promised that he intended to use his new powers to promote economic recovery. But this promise was empty.

Hitler continued to strengthen his grip on power by both legal and illegal means. The first concentration camps for dissenting politicians were built. The SA (*Sturmabteilung* or Storm Troop), the party's hit team, was used as a special police force. There were random arrests, mail and phone services were monitored, unions disbanded, and all parties, except the ruling Nazi Party, were banned. The national-socialist one-party state was established. At the end of June and beginning of July 1934, Hitler took murderous action to eliminate political opponents. Over two hundred victims from all over Germany were shot without trial.

When this caused unrest among the German population, Hitler went on the air to defend his actions, calling them *Staatsnotwehr* (emergency state self-defense), which he had ordered as the "Highest Lord Justice." He warned anyone who might raise a hand to strike against the state that this would mean certain death. From this point onward Hitler held the executive, legislative, and judicial powers in his hand.

Only Hindenburg, president of the German Reich, could theoretically have unseated Hitler, but he died in August 1934, and Hitler immediately grabbed the vacant office, calling himself "*Führer* and chancellor." Through this illegal act, he also became head of the German army (*Reichswehr*). This was in addition to heading the SA and his growing private army, the SS (*Schutzstaffel* or Protective Squadron), which was sworn in personally to follow his every order. From this point on, all organizations, right down to local glee clubs or gardening groups, were under the direct control of the Nazis. Propaganda Minister Joseph Goebbels preached the "national socialist worldview" to all Germans. The secret police (*Gestapo*) were everywhere. The number of concentration camps kept growing.

Hitler increased his grip on the German youth. Beginning at age ten, they were organized as *Jungvolk*, from fourteen and up as "Hitler Youth" and eighteen and older as *Reichsarbeitsdienst* (Reich Work Force), SA, SS, or as soldiers in the army. Parents had practically no say in the education of their children. The official churches were initially appeased, but from about 1934 on, they were persecuted like anybody that tried to elevate God or any other power above almighty Hitler. Schools, universities, and artists were all "put into lockstep," allowed to function only if they didn't question Nazi ideology.

In economic matters, Hitler duped many Germans by promoting road construction (the *Autobahn*); they didn't realize that these projects, along with the push for arms buildup, prepared the way for military aggression against Germany's neighbors. Jews were banned from the business world, and their possessions were confiscated. The national debt was approaching bankruptcy, but no one dared say anything about it publicly. Hitler didn't care about these matters, because he intended to fill Germany's coffers by attacking and exploiting foreign countries.

Those who did not cheer for Hitler or believe his rhetoric were intimidated and often disheartened. Most people conformed and did not protest, even when they observed the ever-increasing pressure on their Jewish neighbors. In 1935, the Nuremberg "Race Laws" were passed, and three years later, in the *Reichskristallnacht*, Jews were systematically slain, abducted, thrown into prison, and and their stores were plundered and burned.

Women were encouraged to become housewives and to bear many children; most of them did not realize that they were being used as tools to give birth to tomorrow's soldiers.

Hitler's foreign policy was just as radical as his domestic policy. At first he had little resistance, because the Germans had unjustly been made responsible for the First World War and had had to cede numerous territories to the victors. (Neither the Russians nor the Americans had signed the Treaty of Versailles.) Hitler tried to achieve a "revision" to the peace treaty, which was valid by all standards of international law. But mainly he was trying to gain time for his rearmament.

A first step was the 1933 withdrawal of Germany from the League of Nations, the predecessor of the United Nations, in order to hide the illegal scope of rearmament. In 1934, Hitler made a pretense of being a "peace lover" by signing a ten-year non-aggression pact with Poland. It lasted only five years. In 1935, when the population of the Saarland, under French administration, voted to be reconnected to the German Reich, Hitler claimed it as proof of the success of his politics.

That year, Hitler reinstituted compulsory military service, even though this was explicitly forbidden by the Treaty of Versailles. At this point it would have been possible for the victorious powers to remove Hitler by military force, but all that happened were lame protests and a warning to not let something like this happen again.

The next violation was the occupation of the Rhine area, which according to the peace treaty was off limits for any German military. The British were hoodwinked with a treaty limiting German naval power, which was meaningless because Hitler never contemplated an attack on the British navy.

Hitler made friends with the fascist leaders of Spain and Italy and was able to test his new weapons in the Spanish Civil

War, from 1936 through 1939. Contrary to his own racial policies, he also made overtures toward the Japanese, hoping that they would be able to draw American attention away from him in a coming war.

Using promises and military threats, Hitler managed to manipulate the vote in Austria, his homeland, so that country chose to be annexed to the new German empire, the *Anschluss*. This was the background for the popular musical, *The Sound of Music*.

In 1938, Hitler demanded that Czechoslovakia yield the Sudetenland, an area with a predominantly German population. The British did precisely the wrong thing: they chose the politics of appeasement, hoping to quiet Hitler down. They saw to it that the Munich Agreement ceded those territories to him.

Hitler then signed a treaty promising to leave the rest of Czechoslovakia alone. Only six months later, German troops invaded Prague, chased out the government, and annexed the rest of the country.

Up to this point, Hitler had wagered the highest stakes and won every time. Finally, the French and British understood that they were dealing with a liar and cheat, and they made it clear that another such step would mean war.

Before moving ahead with his agenda, Hitler tried to prevent having a war on two fronts by signing a non-aggression pact with Russia. In a secret addition to the treaty, Hitler and Stalin agreed that in the case of a German invasion of Poland, Russia would receive part of that country as booty.

With these precautions made, Hitler undertook his planned attack. Disregarding the non-aggression pact, he invaded Poland, hoping that, once again, there would be no international resistance. This time he was wrong. When German troops invaded Poland on September 1, 1939, Great Britain and France, who had defense treaties with Poland, declared war on Germany, making it clear, however, that they could not intervene immediately.

The German word *blitzkrieg*, "lightning war," was coined to describe the campaign against Poland. It was over in less than three weeks. Next, Germany overran Denmark with no resistance, followed by Norway and France.

Great Britain was attacked by the German *Luftwaffe* (air force), but it was not conquered.

Because of Hitler's alliance with Italy, he supported the Italian campaign in the Balkans, and German troops overran Yugoslavia and Greece.

Finally, on June 22, 1941, the German army began a brutal invasion of Russia, again in defiance of the non-aggression pact. This time, though, there was no *blitzkrieg*. The Germans were mired down before reaching Moscow, due to an early, heavy winter.

When Germany's ally, Japan, attacked the US Pacific fleet at Pearl Harbor, without a declaration of war, America entered the action. Hitler believed that the US would be primarily occupied with Japan, but he was mistaken. The Allies' battle slogan was "Germany first!"

This was the first so-called "total war" in modern history, in which civilians were not spared in any way.

The Russian city of Stalingrad was the pivotal turning point for German forces. In North Africa, large numbers of German troops were captured, and in sea battles the allied forces gained superiority. Goebbels, minister of propaganda, goaded the German people to persevere. Having been lied to about the true condition of the war effort, East Germans tried frantically to escape from the advancing Russian troops. Millions died. Subsequently the Russians forced Poles to resettle in areas deserted by the fleeing Germans, while at the same time annexing Polish territory for Russia.

The machinery of the "final solution" of the Jewish problem worked right down to the last weeks of the war. Approximately six million Jews were annihilated in the gas chambers of concentration camps, primarily in Auschwitz. Many other "undesirables" were also murdered: Communists, Socialists, homosexuals, union members, officers, Christian pastors, gypsies, and disabled people. *Most of the Germans didn't find out what really happened behind the walls of the concentration camps until after the war was over.*

There were several assassination attempts against Hitler, but they all failed. The best-known resistance fighters were the Scholl siblings and Graf von Stauffenberg. Hitler ordered their executions.

The *Volkssturm*, made up of old men and German youth, proved unable to halt the advancing Allied troops. Hitler shot himself on April 30, 1945, in his bunker in Berlin. On May 8, the Germans signed the unconditional surrender.

Japan did not give up the fight as hopeless until after atomic bombs were dropped on Hiroshima and Nagasaki. The Japanese empire capitulated on September 2, 1945.

In World War I, about five percent of the dead were civilians. In World War II, civilians made up about fifty percent of the victims. In all, some fifty-five million people died in Europe and Asia.

# PART 1

## 1936 – 1943
## BIRTH TO BOMBS

*Many people bury their memories so they don't have to deal with the pain. For whatever reason, my mother buried hers. I was hard-pressed to get any stories from her. She was not one who shared easily. However, one night was different. It was many years after the war, in 1987, and I was visiting my family in Germany. I felt there were things Mother and I needed to talk about, and I pressed for discussion. I was pleasantly surprised when we stayed up until the wee hours sharing memories.*

*This is my journey: a journey of a German girl during the Hitler regime.*

### INTRODUCTION

On February 28, 2008, sitting on my sunny porch overlooking my lazy river, I made the decision to write my story. Of course, it's not actually my river. It's the Siuslaw, which runs through Florence, Oregon. If anyone owns the river, it would be the Native Americans. The rest of us who enjoy the flow are immigrants.

    I am an immigrant. I was born in Germany and survived World War II. I escaped the Allied bombing and fled the Russians; endured refugee camps, poverty, and near starvation. My childhood was filled with terror, and my teenage years were full of angst. I was sustained by the hope of a better life in America.

The first time I was asked to put my life story in writing was fifty years ago. I came to the United States in 1956, at age nineteen, and less than two years later I married an American citizen. At that time, I attended night school to learn how to gain citizenship. In those days, the mandatory first step toward becoming a citizen was to learn English. My classmates spoke different languages, but the teacher was drawn to my story. He said if I would take the time to record it, he would ask his students to write and compile it. But I wasn't interested. I was young, busy, pregnant, and, quite frankly, bored with the class. I had studied English in Germany for six years and was proficient in both reading and writing my second language. I felt I had better things to do so I dropped out of the class.

Twenty-three years passed before I applied for citizenship. Jimmy Carter was running for president and I wanted to be able to vote. I read an article he had written in a magazine, about his aspirations in life. He mentioned that he couldn't imagine himself starting any day without going to the Lord Jesus, not just the God everyone believes in, for counsel. Just knowing that he had a real relationship with the Lord convinced me that I wanted someone like him to lead our country. That was the impetus that finally motivated me to become a citizen

Not being a citizen had never bothered me before. I carried my green card, paid my taxes, obeyed the law, and went to register at the post office every first of January. No job was denied me except a government job that I had no intentions to apply for anyway.

Since that night school class, I have been asked to tell my story many times. From 1979 to 1985, when I lived in California's San Joaquin Valley, I frequently shared my testimony in churches, clubs, schools, and other venues.

Once, on an airplane, I was carrying a leather-tooled purse that bore the inscription "Jesus is Lord." I was always very bold in sharing my faith, especially after I became intimately acquainted with Him. The man sitting next to me was the owner of a Christian publishing house. We had a very interesting conversation during the flight. He gave me his business card and brochure and said that if I was ever ready to write my story, I should give him a call.

My husband, Larry, picked me up at the airport, and I told him about my conversation with the publisher. I had prayed, "Lord, if this is Your will, let him say yes." But Larry said no and offered no explanation. So, I let it go.

Years later, when my dear friend Merrillin approached me and offered to help me write my story, I said, "Yes." I was in my seventies, and there wasn't much time left. I believed it was the Lord's will. We agreed to make it a joint venture, and that is how this little book came to be.

This is how my story started…

## SOME FAMILY HISTORY

My mother passed away in 1992, and my father outlived her by another fourteen years. I am certain that they are both with the Lord now, and so I can say with confidence "Hallelujah!" and tell my story without fear of offending them.

Mother was born on May 5, 1912. Her name was Anna Wilde, and she had seven brothers and one sister. Her father lost his life in World War I, and her mother raised nine children on her own. My grandmother was a very devout Baptist Christian, but I can hardly remember her as I was very little when she was still alive. We never saw her during the war years, and she immigrated to Detroit after the war, dying there at the age of eighty-nine.

Aunt Frieda, my mother's older sister, told me that my mother was very spoiled because she was the second to youngest of the nine children. I don't know if my mother was spoiled, but I do know she was a mystery to me. I loved her very much, but she was strong-willed, aloof, and hard to please.

One of my most interesting ancestors was my mother's grandfather. He was rich, lived comfortably on his huge farm, and drove a carriage with six horses. I imagined a romantic story, but in reality, his life didn't end happily. My mother's grandfather had a weakness for card playing and gambling and he lost his entire fortune. As a consequence, he hung himself. My mother spoke of him with a great deal of resentment. She was angry that her grandfather's decisions had left the family in dire poverty. Poverty was the bane of her existence. Most of what I learned of family history was shared by my father, Horst Wollin. He was willing to answer my questions while my mother was reluctant to divulge anything, not even anything personal. She never asked me about myself, what I was feeling, whether I was happy or sad—not when I was a child and neither when I was an adult. She never shared anything from her heart.

They say wisdom comes with age. As I grew older I gained a more empathetic understanding of her nature. When she was twenty-one, my mother fell in love with a young man who left her and married another woman. The rejection must have been traumatic for her. A short time later, while on vacation, she met my father. I imagine he was a good catch; blue eyes, tall, dark, handsome, and smart! After the vacation, they returned to their respective homes and corresponded by letter. Within only six months, in what must have been an emotional rebound, she married him.

The marriage was not happy. My father told me she said she never loved him. As I observed them, I came to believe that. When I was a teenager and we lived in cramped quarters after the war, it was easy to hear their arguments. My mother suffered from their tense relationship, but so did my father and the rest of the family, as we watched my father desperately try to buy her love.

My father was born illegitimate on May 31, 1911, to his beautiful mother, Elise. She was adventurous and sometimes rather wild. How funny it seemed that my mother, whose name was Wilde, was anything but, and it was Elise who actually was wild! My father's mother had a wonderful father, a tailor by trade, hardworking, honest, kind, and devoted to his family. When he learned of his daughter's pregnancy, he warned the rest of the family not to speak negatively or harshly about this to her. In fact, I think his other daughter also got pregnant out of wedlock.

In 1911's society, pregnancy out of wedlock was a terrible thing. But his love for his daughter and her son, my father, was unwavering, and that made all the difference.

In those days, the stigma against unwed mothers kept the tailor and his family from going to church. Nonetheless, this man of character and kindness kept a framed picture on his shop wall, embroidered with Romans 12:12: *"Rejoice in hope, be patient in tribulation, hold on to prayer."* My father remembered seeing that verse all the time when he was growing up. Thanks to my friend Gisela, I have that same verse now, embroidered and framed.

Although my father was not brought up in church, he was given a foundation in the Christian faith. He made the decision that when he got married, he would marry a "religious" woman who would raise his children accordingly. In that respect, he made a good marriage with my mother; she was very "religious."

When my father was about eight, his mother married Walter Wollin. Elise bore him a daughter, and Walter adopted my father. But Walter was not a good man. In fact, when I was ten years old, he tried to molest me.

Elise and Walter were both musically gifted. He played the harmonica, and they both loved to party. Alcohol flowed freely, fights were frequent, and on occasion Walter struck Elise. My father left home at age seventeen because he couldn't stand to see the abuse his mother received.

After he left, my father lived alone in a very modest cold-water apartment above a butcher shop, where he learned the trade of bookkeeping. He was very smart, but his stepfather would not buy the books he needed to go on to higher education, even when he had been awarded a full scholarship. My father resented this neglect and lack of support, but he didn't let it hold him back. He became an autodidact and taught himself well. As he pursued his studies, he learned to love the English language.

In December 1934, at ages twenty-three and twenty-two, my father and mother were married and moved to Stettin, at that time referred to as "The Suburb of Berlin." I had always thought of Stettin as a small town, but that was not the case. Even then Stettin's population was over 350,000. My father found a job in Hitler's Voluntary Labor Service. Room and board were provided, and my father was paid twenty-five cents an hour. Unfortunately, after my parents were married, my father was compelled to join the Nazi Party in order to secure a bookkeeping job.

## HITLER RISES

Hitler had begun construction of the *Autobahn* freeway system, and Germany's citizens were elated because many jobs were being created. Some churches even proclaimed that Hitler had been sent by God. There followed six years of peace, prosperity, and hardly any unemployment, my parents told me. No criminal activity was tolerated, and order and high morals were held in great regard. Of course, it was later discovered that these values were not practiced by the regime, but integrity and honor were preached.

In addition, the regime sought to instill the ideal of German superiority. In 1933, freedom of speech began to disappear, and because of one-sided regime media reports in pamphlets and newspapers, on the radio, and at political meetings, hatred began to take root in the hearts of many Germans toward the Jews.

Then, in September 1939, Hitler declared he would free the Germans who lived in Poland. He claimed that the Poles were aggressive, and in turn staged his *Blitzkrieg*, or "lightning war," against Poland. France and England demanded that Hitler withdraw his troops, and that was the beginning of the end. In 1940, the first heavy bombings over Germany began.

## CHILDREN ARE BORN INTO THE WOLLIN FAMILY

Back to 1935, my brother Manfred was born. We always called him Fred. I came along one year later in December 1936. When it was obvious my mother was pregnant, my step-grandfather commented with great disdain, "There she goes again, with her big paunch." I never felt wanted or loved—from birth, I guess.

Three and a half years passed until the next child was born. My father contracted tuberculosis and was sent to a sanatorium from March to September 1939. This was not as unfortunate as it sounds; it was rather the providence of God because it kept my father from being drafted and sent to the front lines during the ensuing years of war. He recovered from the illness but never lost the scars on his lungs, and that would significantly impact our future endeavor to emigrate to the United States.

In August 1940, my brother Lothar was born. I was almost four years old, and that is about the time when *my* memories begin.

## SHELTER FROM THE BOMBS

You might say my memories started with a bang because I can recall with great clarity the sirens going off in the middle of the night, and how we would have to grab the baby in his bassinette and flee to the basement bunker for safety. We lived on the ground level of a huge apartment building with four stories and a cellar below. It was known to be the best on the street because it had heavy steel doors that led into the big bunker.

When the sirens went off, my mother would take the bassinette and carry it to the basement. I never understood why she didn't leave it and just take the baby; the bassinette had a high canopy that made it very difficult to carry. What funny little things we remember! Anyway, this procedure became a frequent routine.

As a result of the bombings, our apartment building was damaged several times, and we would have to leave for a few weeks until it was repaired. The American planes flew over Stettin on the way to Berlin. In the beginning, they dropped bombs randomly over large areas, and later they concentrated on one section at a time, like slicing pieces of pie, in order to wipe out whole regions. During the initial three years of bombings, we never knew when the next aerial attack would come. Berlin was hit even more severely than we were.

## SEASIDE TRIPS AND MISCHIEVOUS SIBLINGS

I do have some pleasant memories of our time in Stettin. Since we lived close to the Baltic Sea, we would frequently take Sunday outings, traveling by streetcar to the northern coast. I remember the fish markets down by the pier where I learned to enjoy all sorts of fish, including herring, flounder, and eel. I recall the day my mother made her first attempt at frying eel and invited us children to watch. The eel flopped in the frying pan, jumping all over the place. I was horrified! Were we really going to eat that? My mother assured me the eel was dead, that its movements were just muscle reflexes.

    I liked fish all right, but I hated milk. I can still see myself sitting on a kitchen chair with my mother across from me, trying to feed me milk soup with dumplings. "Just the dumplings," I begged. "If I drink the milk, I will throw up." Looking back, I obviously had an allergic reaction to dairy.

    It amazes me how many memories I still have of the six years we lived in Stettin. I can even remember our address—Oberwick 24a—and the thoughts I had and how I acted back then. I was a clever child and knew how to get my own way. I remember playing with some kids in a backyard in a sandbox and on swings, and I overheard some women talking nearby. My mother called me into the house to say, "I saw you standing there listening to those two women talking. That's not polite, and I don't want you to do it again." I agreed. Not long after, Mother saw me doing the same thing. "I was watching you, and you did it again," she said. So, I replied, "No, Mutti, this time there weren't *two* women, there were *three*." I suppose I was a bit precocious and seemed to know when I had Mutti in a pickle. Sometimes, this worked to my advantage, and other times…

Mother forbade my brother Fred and me to play cards, probably because of her grandfather who had squandered his wealth by gambling. "Don't ever let me catch you even *touching* any cards!" she warned.

Well, I figured out a way to get around that. We asked the other children to hold the cards for us, and we simply pointed to the cards we wanted and asked them to put them down. A woman in the neighborhood discovered our trickery, thought it was clever, and distracted our mother from finding out. I guess Fred and I held the aces!

The famous Fred and Ginger had nothing on Fred and Dorothea! We certainly had our adventures—and misadventures. One day Fred and I were sitting on the living room windowsill. We had been left at home alone, which happened quite often in Germany; it's rather astonishing to recall how parents would simply leave their children to go shopping or to run errands! Fred and I had nothing to do, and we were bored. I got the brilliant idea that we both needed haircuts.

My mother was a very talented seamstress; she was a whiz with thread and fabric, sewing, knitting, crocheting, and needlepoint. Her sewing machine was across the room and on top was a pair of big scissors. I picked up the scissors and proceeded to cut Fred's hair. When I finished, he cut mine. When my mother returned, she was horrified at what we had done. We could have cut ourselves with the razor-sharp scissors, or poked each other's eyes out, or fallen on the scissors and stabbed ourselves!

Needless to say, we were punished this time. Mother laid into us with good, hard spankings. We were also punished for a long time by the sight of ourselves in weird haircuts.

But that didn't stop our shenanigans. Another day when my mother left Fred and me home alone, we passed the time in the kitchen. There was a clock on the wall above the kitchen table. I decided it wasn't showing the right time, so I came up with the idea that my brother should climb up and change it. "Take this chair and put it on the table and climb on top to see if you can reach the clock," I ordered. Fred did as I had asked, but he wasn't high enough to reach the hands on the clock. I had a solution. "Put this little footstool on top of the chair and then climb up." He followed my suggestion, and it worked. He adjusted the time. At least we thought it was properly adjusted. Something must have gone awry because we were found out and punished. My mother guessed I had instigated the clock caper, so I got the bigger whipping.

There was a time when Fred got his comeuppance. It was a Sunday, and we were preparing to leave on an outing. Fred was about seven, I was six, and Lothar was two and a half. My mother had the boys ready and told them to go outside with clear instructions to Fred to hold Lothar's hand and wait for us. When we joined the boys, we found Fred intently watching some workers repair something in the street; Lothar was nowhere in sight! Fred had not been paying attention and let go of Lothar's hand, so Lothar had wandered off as any two-year-old would. We anxiously searched for several hours, fearing what might have happened to little Lothar.

In those days, there were no telephones with which to call for help. We had to go from house to house asking questions, hoping people would relay our message. Only after doing all we could would it be proper to contact the police.

About four hours later a Hitler Youth brought Lothar back. This Hitler Youth had found Lothar with some stranger, figured out where he belonged. Of course, we were all relieved.

Mother discovered Fred hidden under the kitchen table, shaking with fear like a scared little animal. She grabbed him and yanked him out. This time he got a hard whipping with a belt. I thought this was unjust because Fred knew he had done wrong and had already suffered greatly. I cried and begged for Mother to be merciful, but she didn't stop. She was a very stern disciplinarian.

## HITLER YOUTH

Hitler and his regime were not living what they taught, and the hypocrisy in lifestyle was only exposed after the war ended. Debauchery, greed, lust for power, and sexual immorality were the exclusive, hidden lifestyle of what Hitler deemed his elite cohort of commanders. It was easy to fool innocent, good citizens into believing that all was well and virtuous.

Hitler Youth were somewhat like Boy Scouts or Pathfinders: boys could join when they were about thirteen; they wore uniforms and received strict discipline. They were nice young boys. The Hitler Youth had an impeccable reputation at that time because they were so well behaved, helpful, and honest.

Looking back in history at the Nazi regime it is amazing how the deception was widespread and very effective. These young boys and girls were brought up under a strict, ethic code of honesty, integrity, and helpfulness, none practiced by the leaders. The question *How could the public not have known better?* is often asked. This could not happen now; or could it? A movie produced in 1981 called *The Wave* would prove otherwise and showed the dangers and capacity to brainwash young minds. It is a riveting account of a class of students being slowly influenced by powerful deceptions.

My brother Lothar, a history and German language professor, wrote his thesis on the Nazi regime. He told me when *The Wave* was shown in Germany a deathly silence followed among the students, caused by the overwhelming effect the movie had on its viewers. Lothar has dedicated his life to fighting against Neo-Nazism and says, "If just one young person is kept from falling into the trap, it's all worth it."

One time after the war my Aunt Annelies told us how at one of the parades through town she met Adolf Hitler. She said he stopped to receive a bouquet of white roses from her. He took her hand, pulled her very close, and said, "*Vielen Dank*," thanking her, and she described his eyes as "penetrating her very spirit like a burning fire." Extremely beautiful and innocent, at nineteen years old she was mesmerized and almost fainted. She claimed she didn't wash her hand for a week. Such was the devilish deception with the youth.

Heinz Radloff, the handsome husband she married in 1940, the same year my little brother Lothar was born, was sent to the front lines and missing in action until the day she died. Aunt

Annelies kept watching for his return and never got over losing him to the cruel winter in Russia in 1944 where thousands of soldiers froze to death. Raising two beautiful daughters alone, she became another victim of the devastation of Hitler's war.

In retrospect, I know that the majority of average German citizens, like my parents, were brainwashed by Nazi propaganda. There were no truthful news reports or radio broadcasts, and TVs did not exist. Everything was censored and under Nazi control. Most people did not know that Germany was the aggressor, and it was easy to convince civilians that all the bombings were from our enemies and undeserved, all unthinkable in today's civilized, media-controlled populations. Economic growth and law and order were the Nazi message; far from the truth.

## OUR APARTMENT IN STETTIN

If I had to, I could draw a detailed picture of our apartment in Stettin. We lived on the ground floor of a four-story building in a nice unit. There were big front windows in the living room with a view of the street. I especially loved the big brick oven—*Kachelofen*—decorated with beautiful tile work and used to heat the house with coal. I enjoyed one of the oven's other uses: baking apples. I can still savor the warm, sweet flavor.

The children's bedroom was to the right of the living room. There were many nights when my sleep was interrupted by a party in the living room. My parents liked to entertain while my father was still with us. I could hear the guests enjoying themselves, and I wanted to be in there with them. But all my attempts to join in were thwarted. Hoping to be among the grown-ups, if only to be trotted through the living room out to the toilet down the hall, I told my mother I needed to pee. This time she saw through my ploy and brought a pot to the bedroom to use if I really had to go. I didn't want to sit down in the dark, so I went back to bed.

As I said, the toilet was down the hallway from our apartment. Each floor had a chemical toilet, and ours was out in the hall and down some steps. It was dark and smelled really bad.

I hated it and never went there by myself. The other renters on our floor had to use the same toilet. To this day, I am wary about public bathrooms, but that's just the way it was in those days.

Of course, we didn't have a bath or shower, either. Instead, we had a large tub in the kitchen. We filled it with water and took a bath once a week. We had little washbasins for everyday use. They say cleanliness is next to godliness, but when I was growing up, it was not easy keeping clean.

## "UNCLE HITLER"

In our living room, there was a picture of Adolf Hitler on the wall. We called him "Uncle Hitler." We didn't go to church in those days, but we prayed traditional prayers at meals and bedtime. I remember our evening prayer: *"Bless Mutti and Vati and all the others . . . and bless 'Uncle Hitler.'"* I never asked why we referred to Hitler as "Uncle"; this was simply the traditional way to address adults in the German culture.

## BAKERY SELLS AMERICANS

Right across the street from our apartment was a bakery, and every now and then I would get a nickel to buy some "Americans." No, it was not a cannibal thing; what we called Americans was a pastry that was flat, somewhat like a pancake, but baked, with a lot of frosting on top. It was delicious! Americans were my favorites.

One day my mother said that tomorrow afternoon we would see some "Americans" come through. Of course, I didn't ask any questions, but my imagination created some kind of space people with round bodies and sticks for arms—stick figures like I had seen in children's books. I thought the Americans might be shaped like my favorite pastry! The next day I climbed on my windowsill, which was my favorite place to sit, and waited for the Americans to come through. When they finally appeared, I was disappointed. They were nothing like I had imagined. They were just a bunch of weary, sad-looking prisoners of war, herded through our town like injured animals. Most disappointing of all, *they looked just like us!*

"Why did you say they were Americans?" I asked my mother. "They look just like us." Her explanation was my first lesson on humanity and war, and it led me to wonder: *Why? If we all look alike, and if we are all the same, why on earth are we fighting each other?* I wasn't able to reconcile this, but I didn't ask any more questions because I knew I wouldn't get any answers.

## A FEARFUL ATTACHMENT TO MOTHER

It was around this time that fear crept into my heart and became a constant companion, causing me to develop an unhealthy attachment to my mother. A large wardrobe sat at the end of the hall in our apartment, and from time to time I would retreat there to hide among the coats that bore my mother's scent. As I huddled there, I cried, wondering what life would be like if she died. This exaggerated attachment—which later became more pronounced—brought me a lot of pain, and I can't imagine it was easy for her, either. Because we never knew what the next day would bring, my fears became an integral part of my life.

## PERPETUAL BOMBINGS

My earliest memories were from 1940 when I was almost four years old. Baby brother Lothar was born that year, and the bombings became more frequent. Sirens and evacuating to the bunker became a way of life. One never knew what section would be chosen for complete annihilation. Although Stettin lay nearly one hundred kilometers from Berlin, the British pilots viewed it as a suburb of the big city, and since we were located on their designated flight path, we were subject to continual air raids.

At first, the RAF (Royal Air Force) attempted to only bomb military and industrial targets during daytime raids. However, in 1942 the British abandoned their "precision bombing" strategy and took the fateful step to de-house the German people, which they hoped would shatter their morale and will to continue the war. The attacks systematically took place, with whole areas targeted for slicing, like pieces of pie. These targeted bombings would start fires in each of the areas, which would merge together and create a massive firestorm, sucking up oxygen and generating powerful winds. Many who were not burned to death were asphyxiated in underground bomb shelters.

On one occasion a stray bomb hit our street. We were evacuated for two or three weeks for repairs on our apartment house and possibly others that I was too young to recall. This would pale in comparison to what was yet to come. Our luck would soon run out.

## THE LAST ATTACK

The final, most devastating attack came in 1943, in the middle of the night. I was six years old and the first to hear the sirens. It was the day before Hitler's birthday, and the streets were beautifully decorated with flags and flowers everywhere.

A parade was planned to blanket the streets, a celebration of Hitler's birthday. These rallies and parades were a common occurrence in those days. Thousands would show up to be roused to a frenzy by patriotic speeches by the Elite Nazi Party with loudspeakers and bands blaring. Our street was broad and could easily accommodate the crowds that would gather for the parades. I was never allowed to see the parades because they were mostly at night and my mother would put us to bed. But those beautiful visions of our street accompanied me in bed, with anticipation for the following day of festivities.

"Uncle Hitler's" picture still hung on the wall. That evening we put him in our evening prayers as usual. Back then none of us fathomed how dreadful he was. Today it seems unthinkable that we did not know.

That night, as soon as I heard the sirens, I called for my mother. She came to me and said I was dreaming and everything would be all right. But the sirens went off again.

Fortunately, my father was on leave from the army so he

was home to help. All three of us children had measles, so our parents did not make us get dressed but picked us up, wrapped us in blankets, and carried us down to the bomb shelter. A *big, black handbag,* with all of our papers, was always ready to go and my mother grabbed it in our mad dash.

The airplanes had been diverted from Berlin, presumably because they had been met with a counterattack, and the pilots had selected Stettin as their next bombing target. The first bombardment resulted in heavy damage, breaking the pipes and blowing soot everywhere. People started flooding the shelter. That elderly, deaf, lame couple from our building had not heard the sirens right away, and when they did, the bombs were already falling. They lived on the second floor and lost their footing on the stairs, tumbled all the way down, and landed at the doors to the bunker. They were the last ones taken in.

The shelter was full. More people begged to be admitted, but we had to turn them away. I felt awful, knowing that there were frightened people outside, desperate for help, but we couldn't let them into the already overcrowded bunker, or we would all risk suffocating.

We held wet cloths over our mouths to have some relief as we breathed. Many cried. The old couple wanted a mirror to see how badly they had been bruised from their fall, but no one wanted to give them one. They were a frightful sight to behold, and to us children, already afraid of them, they looked like monsters.

Before the bunker doors were locked, my father went up for a walk-through of the apartment. Upon his return, he told us that the cups in the cupboards were dancing. I think he was trying to cheer us up. I did find it amusing, and for a while, I was distracted, picturing dancing cups and dishes running away with spoons, like in the old nursery rhyme.

The guards stopped by our bunker from time to time to report the state of things outside. At last, one of the guards warned that the situation was grim, and said it was time to decide to go or stay. "If you stay," he said, "I can't come back to tell you what's happening. This is the last time I will be here."

My father decided we needed to go. He carried me; my mother picked up my little brother and the *big, black handbag* that held our papers. My older brother walked beside us. I was scared but glad to get out of the cramped shelter. I looked forward to the beautiful decorations, flowers, and flags I had admired the day before from my seat on the windowsill.

But as we stepped into the street, I saw nothing but raging fire, black smoke, and sheets of flames engulfing the tall apartment buildings on both sides of the narrow street, crushing the innocence of the previous day's vision.

We found a pathway down the middle. Beams from burning buildings crashed around us, and my brother Fred got singed by some of the sparks.

That night I lost my ability to speak.

## REST BESIDE A CREEK

After we had passed through the burning buildings, we arrived at a little clearing in a park, alongside a creek. The bombing continued like a huge display of fireworks. One bomb fell on a gasoline factory not far from us, and the explosion lit up the sky. Nevertheless, we were glad to be out in the open, where we could breathe.

Surrounding us were others who had escaped from burning buildings. We shared the camaraderie that is built in the midst of disaster, and we looked out for one another. People noticed that my brothers and I were sick, and they reached out to help by sharing their food and blankets, and finding ways to care for us.

As the night wore on, many others, who had been bombed out of their homes, fled to the park. Everywhere around us were soot-covered faces, some with blank stares, others with expressions of despair. Many children screamed and cried.

The bombing continued through the night. The next morning, we returned to our building to find that it had been completely destroyed, razed to the ground. There was nothing to go back to. Except for our papers, which my mother protected in the *big, black handbag*, we had lost everything.

During the months and years of attacks to come, millions of Germans, many of them women and children, would be killed.

That night, my childhood ended. The struggle to survive began.

# PART 2

## APRIL 1943 - MAY 1947
## FLIGHT

### LOST MEMORIES

Many years later, before my parents passed away, I sat down with them, and we went through a detailed timeline of events from World War II. That's when I realized I had essentially lost an entire year of memories, starting from the day we were bombed out and left homeless.

My parents told me that from April 1943 to April 1944 we traveled from relative to relative. They told me names of some of the towns, including Sinslow and Buetow, where we sought shelter. It was not easy to find help. We had nothing, and few had more. Those who tried to help were limited in what they could offer since they lived in cramped quarters themselves and didn't have accommodations for another family.

I have a clear recollection of only two things during that lost year:

First, for two months I was unable to speak. I was in a state of shock after the fire in the streets. Because there was a great deal of confusion, and everyone was just trying to survive, nobody paid attention, until a few days later when I still hadn't said a word.[1]

---

[1] *Post-traumatic stress disorder, often abbreviated as PTSD, is a complex disorder in which the affected person's memory, emotional responses, intellectual processes, and nervous system have all been disrupted by one or more traumatic experiences. It is sometimes summarized as "a normal reaction to abnormal events." The DSM-IV-TR (the professional's diagnostic manual) classifies PTSD as an anxiety disorder.*

Second, I remember my mother taking me to a woman doctor. I never did find out whether she was a physician, a psychologist, or a psychiatrist. I just sat there while everyone nagged me to talk: "Why don't you just talk? You're going to get in trouble if you don't talk."

But I couldn't speak. I could only shut my eyes and cry. My mind was racing. I wished I could talk, but I couldn't. The "doctor" was no help at all! My brain was just coping the only way it knew how.

Those two months seemed unending. I was frustrated, unable to communicate except by pointing. Suddenly, it was as if God told me that my voice was fighting its way out from under the bombing rubble. I was still alive; I had a future and something to say!

I didn't know much about God then, but I did begin to talk. My vocal cords were raw and rusty, but my ability to speak returned.

I have not been lost for words since.

## MATERNAL ATTACHMENT GROWS

After I had regained my speech and memory, another incident proved traumatic. It involved my brother Lothar. We were in some strange place, and Lothar had been put down for a nap. For whatever reason, he was left alone. He fell asleep but was awakened by the sound of sirens, and he panicked. He must have noticed an open window in the room in which he had been sleeping. The window was close to the ground, accessible to a baby. Lothar must have toddled over and jumped out, plummeting to the ground below. The fall broke his leg.

It was not uncommon for parents to put their children to bed or down for a nap without a babysitter and leave them to run an errand or, even, socialize. I suppose, looking back, it was severely damaging psychologically to do this to children especially during a time of war. This would explain my severe attachment disorder.

His injury was treated, and he was fine, but the event was

traumatic for me. The fear of being alone with blaring sirens and falling to my doom scared me, and the attachment to my mother grew fiercer. I could not let go of her. She had to be within my reach or my sight at all times. If she wasn't, I was engulfed with panic.

## A NEW PLACE TO LIVE: RODENAU IN SCHLESIEN

In 1944, we experienced the Lord's great mercy when we were sent to Rodenau in Schlesien, at that time located on the border of Germany and Czechoslovakia. We moved in with my aunt Hildegard Wilde, my mother's sister-in-law. She and her family lived in that area because my uncle was a border guard. He had been drafted to fight in the war, and we were allowed to stay in his house with Aunt Hilde and her daughters Adelheid and Ute.

Their home was in the country, and we enjoyed a pleasant respite for the months we lived there. Rodenau was a tiny village, far from the fighting, without the constant drone of war planes and sirens that we had experienced for years in Stettin. The only evidence of warfare was news reports on radio and in the newspapers. This time in the countryside gave us rest that we so desperately needed to get well, both mentally and physically. It proved to be utterly crucial to prepare my mother and aunt for what lay ahead.

It was at that time that I came to love country living. We lived among scattered little farms with hardworking, humble people who treated us kindly. The farmers gave us opportunities to experience the bucolic life. We were allowed to feed the animals—pigs, sheep, goats, and calves—and help pick apples from their trees. Since we were used to the city, it was a wonderful, endless adventure.

I remember the huge stork nests atop the farmhouses. We watched them raise their young. These birds were especially fascinating because we had heard the story of storks bringing babies. I knew it was just a story, but I liked the idea of a stork swooping out of the sky and putting a cooing baby in my arms.

Even rain on hot summer days did not keep us from playing outside. One portion of the nearby meadow that lay lower than the rest would fill up after a heavy rain, with warm water like a swimming pool. We had a wonderful time splashing in it.

The farmers used freshly mowed grass to make hay. I will never forget its fresh scent. I loved to roll around in the hay, savoring its aroma. To this day, when I smell freshly mowed grass, I am filled with joy and a sense of safety.

## GOING TO SCHOOL

Fred, our cousins Ute and Adelheid, and I (all of us around ages seven and eight) had a long way to walk to school in the little town next to the village where we lived. This was not a casual stroll to another part of our community. It was possibly a couple kilometers away, and we lost complete contact from the protection of the adults caring for us. Classes were held in a small, old-fashioned building with about four grades in one room. The students were separated by grade level, and we were the little ones, the beginners. We learned to write with chalk on slates, and I practiced my writing at every opportunity. I enjoyed school so much that I looked forward to every day.

Eventually, however, I realized that Fred and I were outsiders in the tight school community. One day our teacher gave us an assignment, and when we had finished, she called on Fred and me to hold up our slates for the class to see. She praised our good work. I think she meant well, but her action backfired because the class became upset. Clearly, the children were not fond of us; they looked on us with disdain since we didn't speak their dialect.

Stettin, where we came from, was a large town and did not have its own dialect; we spoke High German. In Germany, every state, every region, and sometimes even individual cities have their own dialect, and if a new way of speaking is not immediately mastered, one easily stands out as an outsider. Our classmates were uncomfortable with us, and the teacher's compliments turned their irritation to anger. At the end of class,

Fred and I had to run for our lives. If our cousins hadn't been there to protect us, we almost certainly would have been beaten—and all for speaking a different dialect!

After this encounter, we did not want to go to school. I am certain that my mother and aunt went to the school on our behalf to make things right and bring reconciliation, but our bad experience was just an indication of what was to come. Fred and I managed to rise above the situation, but it would not be the last time I was hated for something I could not help.

In all my years in Germany, going to school was mandatory. Whether the country was at war or facing other terrible circumstances, children were always sent to school. This made a significant impact on us and, in the long run, proved to have a positive effect, making us tough and resilient.

## NEEDINESS FOR MOTHER GROWS

My obsessive attachment to my mother continued in spite of the peaceful surroundings we found ourselves in. When one day she suffered heart complications and was to be admitted to the hospital for observation, I went into a panic. I clung to her and couldn't be separated from her. When the adults realized how traumatic it was for me to be apart from my mother, they admitted me to the hospital with her. I was finally able to breathe easily.

On another occasion, my mother had to go to the dentist. Back then, there were no cars or buses, and she had to travel by bicycle. Her appointment was in a neighboring town a good distance away, and I was ordered to stay behind. I couldn't help wailing loudly to protest her going. I sat on a stool and cried bloody murder. My aunt tried in vain to calm me down. She gave me food and toys, but I just sat with my hands folded and my eyes shut tight.

After I had cried my eyes dry, I sat motionless, as though in a coma. I would not talk, eat, or move until my mother returned several hours later. Although my aunt was loving and kind, there was nothing she could do about my fear.

When my mother was near, I was joyful, playful, and at peace. As soon as I felt our closeness threatened, I became hysterical. Her emotional detachment only seemed to hasten my fear of losing her.

## NO ONE TAUGHT ME ABOUT PRAYER

Nobody ever prayed for me or with me in a personal and relational way. As I have said, our family prayers were simple, scripted, and repetitive, such as: "Now I lay me down to sleep, I pray the Lord my soul to keep." When I was an adult, I wondered why this had been my only experience with prayer; after all, my mother had been raised in a Baptist church and had accepted the Lord Jesus as her Savior. Sadly, she never told me about Him. She never took the time to explain or share anything with me about her faith.

That could be part of the reason why, to this day, I share everything and anything about the Lord Jesus with my children and anyone else, so far as they give me the freedom to do so. He is, after all, the most important person who ever lived on this planet.

## A LITTLE LIE IS STILL A LIE

I know parents should never lie to their children, and I hold to that belief because I can recall three significant incidents that took place during our time in Rodenau when I was lied to. There may be those who think that a little lie may not be a big deal, but to a trusting, impressionable child who believes everything he or she is told, little white lies can be harmful. I was very trusting, and I was a "thinker." Even at the age of six or seven, I often pondered and dwelled on deep things.

Since the men were off at war or serving the country elsewhere, my mother and Aunt Hille were left to care for everything. One of their responsibilities was caring for the chickens. My brothers, my cousins, and I enjoyed feeding the chickens and gathering their eggs.

Every so often, chicken was on the dinner menu. That meant a chicken had to be killed. We were allowed to watch our mothers catch a chicken, hold it by its legs, throw it on the chopping block, and chop its head off. I would not have wanted my children to watch this ordeal, but we did.

One time, a chicken got loose after its head had been chopped off. It may have been my mother who let it go, since, as a city girl, she was not used to slaughtering chickens. Anyway, the chicken took off, fluttering about and squirting blood everywhere. We scattered in terror.

When the chicken was finally caught and ceased to move, we helped dunk it in hot water and pull out all its feathers. This was a tedious, stinky task. Once it was completed, the chicken was placed in a pan and roasted until the skin was crisp and browned to perfection.

When it came time to eat, everyone wanted some of the crisp skin, including me. But we were told the skin was not to be consumed by children, and if we ate any, it would stunt our growth.

At that time, I was very petite; in fact, I was very small for a long time. Some of my nicknames were "little carrot" and *Püppchen* (tiny doll), and I remained smaller than most of my peers until I became a teenager. We had to line up by height for PE class, and I was always the last one in the row until a shorter girl joined the class. So, once I heard that chicken skin would stunt my growth, I did not want one bite!

Later on, I was disappointed to find out that what we had been told was nonsense, and I realized the adults probably just wanted the chicken skin for themselves. That was one of those "little lies."

I recall another time I was confronted with one of these fibs. That day, I was running outside and didn't see a rake in my path, the tines sticking up. One of the iron tines pierced the skin between two of my toes. There was blood everywhere, and the pain severe.

There were no doctors in the area, so we had to take care of ourselves. Since I had observed how other small wounds had been treated, I knew that iodine was frequently administered to prevent infection. I also knew that it could sting badly.

I begged my mother not to put any iodine between my toes. I cramped my leg and pulled it under myself to keep it away from the burning liquid. I screamed and fought anyone who tried to touch me. I wish my mother and my aunt had calmly but firmly insisted I stop resisting because it needed to be done to heal the wound. But they went about it another way. They said, "We're not going to do anything. We promise we won't do anything. Just calm down and let us take a look at your toes." So, after many promises and some coaxing, I let down my guard. As soon as I did, however, they grabbed my foot and slathered it with iodine. I was horrified! They had blatantly lied to me!

It makes me think of how differently the Lord deals with us, His children. In the Scriptures, we find very clear and precise instruction about the rules we are to obey, as well as the consequences that will follow if we deviate. We are given freedom to choose, and hopefully, we learn quickly that it is for our own good to follow His instructions.

The third lie I was told profoundly affected my experience of Christmas. I was always the nurturing, motherly type. I loved babies and taking care of children, a desire I was able to fulfill by looking out for little Lothar. I yearned for a baby doll, but they were hard to come by. Somehow, my mother and aunt managed to get ahold of some dolls. One of them was an oversized Barbie-like character composed of celluloid. My mother took to knitting and sewing fancy doll dresses and play clothes for this doll. But I wasn't interested in the Barbie doll; I wanted a baby doll, and my mother knew it. I asked her why she was working on the Barbie doll, and she replied nonchalantly, "Oh, this is a present for your cousin. It's not for you." She assured me repeatedly that it was not for me.

When Christmas came, and I unwrapped my gifts, my present was—you guessed it—the Barbie doll! I was stunned. To make matters worse, my cousin Ute received the baby doll I so longed for.

*(top)* My Mom, Anna Wilde, 1926 (third from left), with her siblings and grandmother Emma. (Grandfather and one brother died in WWI.)

*(left)* My Dad, Horst Wollin, at his confirmation, 1925, in Glauchau, East Germany.

Dad and half-sister, Annelies, 1935, Glauchau, East Germany.

*(top)* Mom and Dad (in the middle), 1935, Schlesien, East Germany.

*(bottom)* Mom's seven remaining brothers in 1926.

*(top)* Mom, brother Fred and me, 1938, Stettin, East Germany.

*(above)* Myself at three years old (when memories begin), 1939, Stettin, East Germany.

*(left)* Eliese Wollin, my beautiful "wild" Grandma at 50 years old, 1941.

1943 wartime family picture: Fred, Mom, Lothar, myself, Dad.
Note: the scratched off portion on Dad's lapel originally
showed a Nazi Swastika lapel pin.

---

Following are photos of the best time of my life
(**1944**, Rodenau, East Germany), nine months break
**after** bombings, **before** fleeing the Russians.

Picking wheat. *(l.-r.)* Adelheid, Fred, Lothar, Ute and me.

*(top, left)* (l.-r.) me, Mom, Fred, Lothar and cousins Ute and Adelheid.

*(top right)* Precious Lothar : "Ich habe eins gefunden!" *("I found one!")*

*(right)* Me helping Mom in the garden.

Last picture before leaving Rodenau (myself on right).

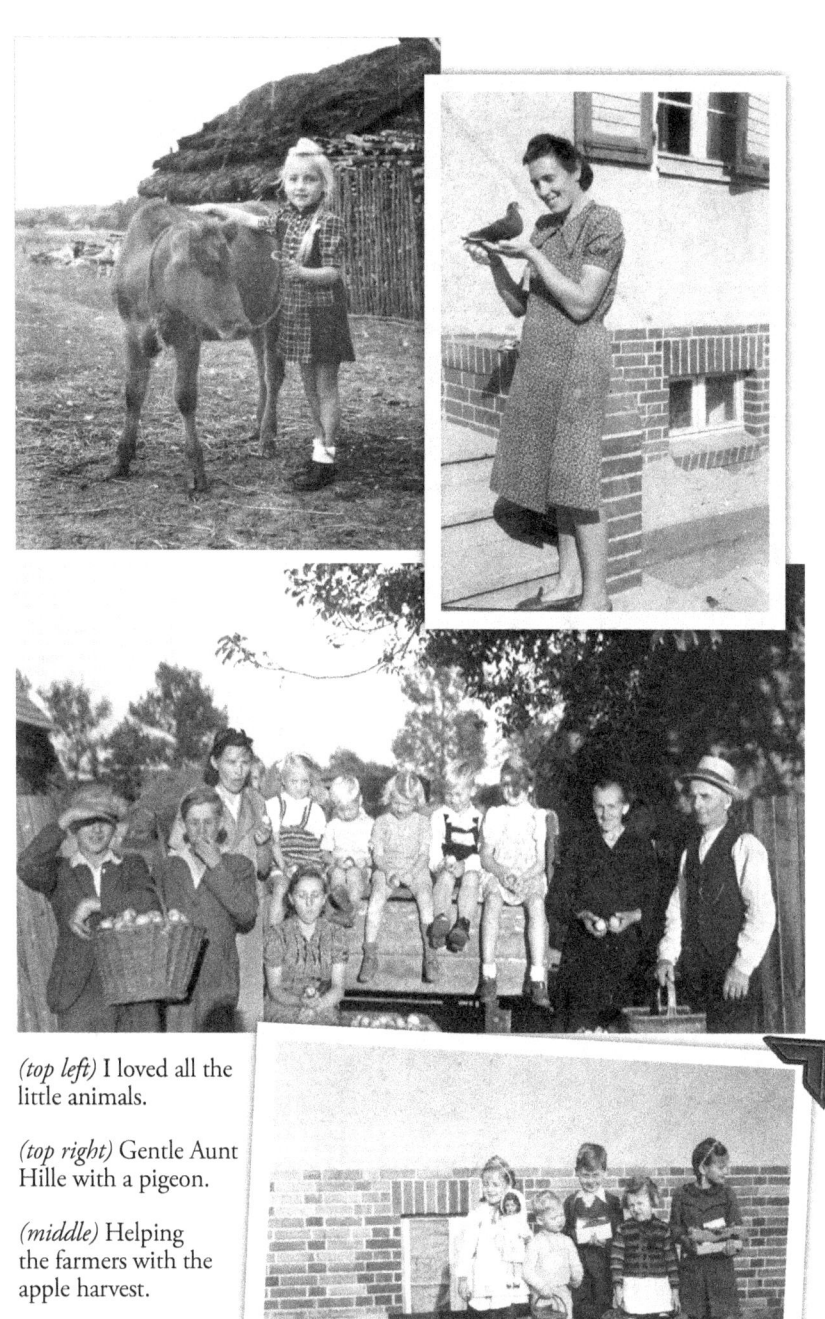

*(top left)* I loved all the little animals.

*(top right)* Gentle Aunt Hille with a pigeon.

*(middle)* Helping the farmers with the apple harvest.

*(right)* Easter – me, Lothar, Fred, Adelheid and Ute.

**1948-1954** Neustadt, Bavaria, West Germany, after the war.

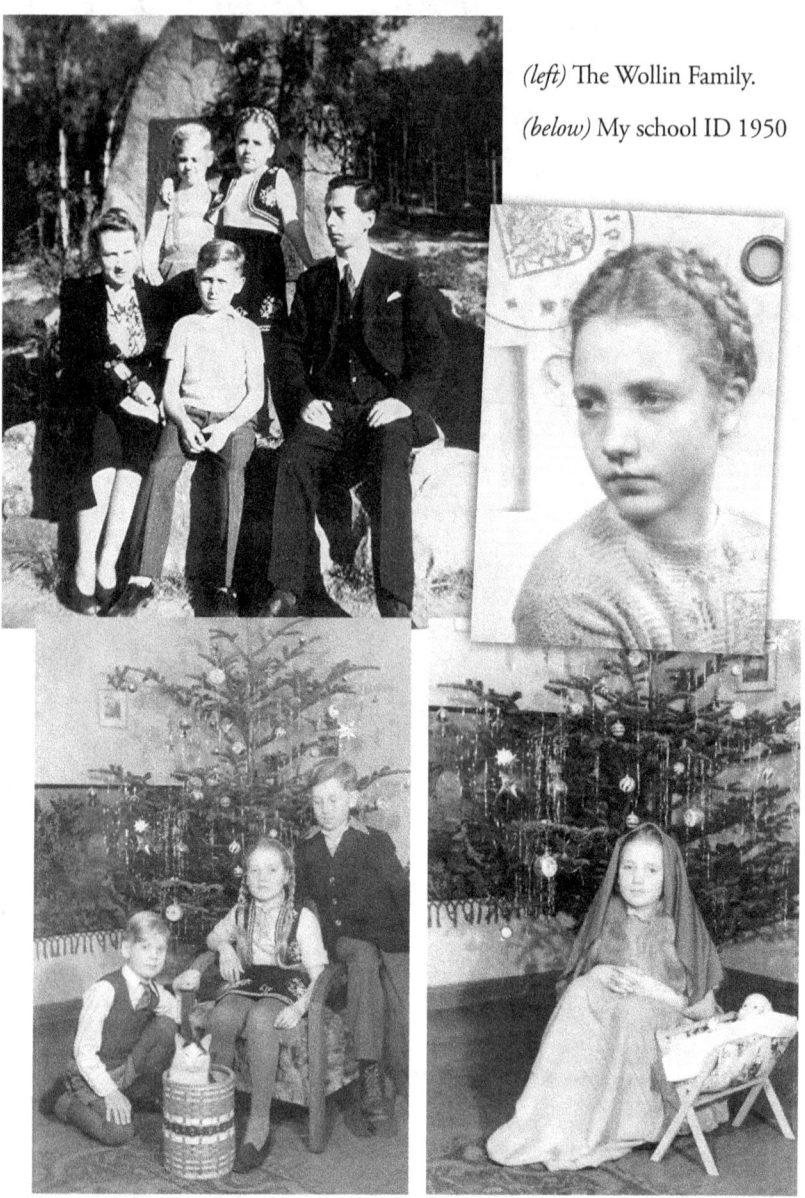

*(left)* The Wollin Family.

*(below)* My school ID 1950

*(above left)* Christmas at our Pastor Hoch's house, 1950.

*(above right)* At our pastor's house, 1950 (I had just played Mary in a Christmas play).

*(above)* Family picture,
just before Martin was born, 1950.

*(below)* Lothar and I with precious baby Martin.

*(left)* "Lumpacivagabundes" school play, 1952, (myself, 4th from left).

*(middle)* Christmas play, (myself, first on right).

*(bottom)* Shakespeare's "Midsummer Night's Dream" (myself, 2nd from left).

*(above)* Christmas, 1954.

*(below)* Graduation, 1954
(myself, 3rd From left).

"Chris," the stranger on train who treated us to our first hamburger.

*(top right)* Clowning around last day on board ship to America, October 2, 1956. The one holding my hand "found" me two years later in Tulare.

*(middle)* New York skyline.

*(right)* Fun is over... what comes next?

**FAST FORWARD 50+ years**

Larry and me at our lakeside home on the Oregon coast; with our 10 grandchildren, for whom I undertook this project.

I had been raised not to complain or to talk back, so I held my tongue, but I was traumatized because my mother had lied to me. As time passed, my cousin let me play with her baby doll. I am a "stickler" for telling the truth, to this day!

A little lie is still a lie. As an adult, I have always made a concerted effort not to do to my children the negative things that were done to me. I have always made it a point to ask them if there is anything in their past that I should ask forgiveness for. Most of all, I have tried my utmost to always be honest with them.

## FATHER DREAMS OF AMERICA

My father and uncle came to visit us only once during our stay in the countryside of Rodenau when they received leave from the army. My father had been assigned to a desk job because he had suffered tuberculosis as a young man. He was also assigned to guard the American prisoners of war. His superiors had told him during his training that he would never make a good soldier because he was not tough enough; they said he handled his gun like a bride on a honeymoon. I think my father laughed at their taunts because he was glad to be out of the line of fire.

He seemed to enjoy guarding the prisoners and was kind to them. He took them out to work in the woods and ensured they were given breaks. On the way back to the barracks, he let them have beer—good, German beer. He even played checkers with them. But his humanity got him in trouble with his superiors and more than once he was transferred to other assignments.

My father's kindness toward the American prisoners blossomed into friendships, even amidst the circumstances of war, and he learned a good deal of the English language. After the war ended, one of the former prisoners, General Love, wrote an affidavit from his home in Washington, D.C., stating that my father should be allowed to immigrate due to the compassion he had shown the prisoners. My father included this affidavit in his immigration application, but it didn't outweigh his bout with tuberculosis, and entry into the USA was denied.

The Lord had different plans for our family and, in the end, it was better that he did not immigrate to the United States.

## TIME TO LEAVE IDYLLIC RODENAU

My life in Rodenau was about to end. I overheard the adults talk about people leaving—not just leaving but fleeing. It was becoming more dangerous for Germans to stay in the east. Soon we, too, would have to go.

Secretly, I hoped this was true. I had an adventurous spirit and rarely felt homesick. Quite the opposite; I longed to know what was out there, far away. Befitting a child, I was innocently ignorant of the horrors that, once again, lie ahead.

On January 14, 1945, the warning came over the radio: "Run! The Russians are coming!" The news reached the weary little community in the village of Rodenau in Schlesien, where we lived in relative peace, except for the humming of scattered war planes. When we heard the call to go, over the radio, we formed a caravan and joined others fleeing the Russians.

Everyone was confused and distraught. My excitement about leaving turned to guilt as I sensed the difficulties ahead. I, after all, had prayed for this chance at adventure. Perhaps this was my fault.

Thank goodness for my level-headed mother! A strong individual, she managed what to take and what to leave behind. We weren't allowed much, just some clothing and personal items. But one thing was essential; the *big, black handbag* with our papers.

In the chaos of this crisis, my aunt almost had a nervous breakdown. She stood in the kitchen, lackadaisically washing wine glasses, oblivious to what was happening. After repeated attempts to get her on track, my mother grabbed her by the shoulders and shook her, insisting, "The situation is urgent! We need to leave immediately!"

My mother's strength was invaluable to our family's survival. Much later, my aunt would affirm that my mother was her tower of strength and she doubted she would have made it without her.

As we prepared to leave, we discovered how quickly people could change. The friendly farmers transformed overnight. They were no longer kind to us, as they had been when we arrived. They selfishly took and did what they wanted for their own survival. I realized that the stress of the situation had filled them more with fear than compassion.

Finally, our wagon train was loaded. Children under eight were crammed under a tarp, atop the belongings, and older kids walked alongside the adults. I was seven, and Fred was eight; I envied him because he was permitted to walk.

The peaceful days were over, and the coming season held the most traumatic and troubling times of the war years.

## OVER THE ICY MOUNTAINS INTO CZECHOSLOVAKIA

It was in the freezing cold winter of 1945 that we were forced to flee the advancing Russian army. I have never understood why the German authorities made us travel over the icy mountain range called Eulengebirge, when they could have sent us directly west into Germany. As it was, our route followed a path southwest through the neighboring country of Czechoslovakia. Nothing took place quite as planned, and for four arduous months we plodded through the dead of a freezing cold, snowy, icy winter. I get chills just thinking about it!

During the trek, it was the little ones who suffered most. I am haunted by the plight of little Lothar, the sweet little boy with curly, blond hair, of whom I was so proud. He and I were riding on the overcrowded wagon. Suddenly he started to cry. "What's the matter?" I whispered. "Are you hurt? Are you afraid? Do you have to pee?" That could have been a possibility since there was hardly ever time for that. The wagon train would not stop during the day; if you got off for any reason, you had to run to catch up.

A crabby, old woman was sitting near us, holding the reins of the horses that pulled our wagon. When Lothar cried, she hollered to make him shut up. He didn't stop, and she screamed again and again. My mother heard the commotion, climbed onto the wagon, and slapped Lothar across the face. He stopped crying, probably in shock. I was appalled, crushed, upset, astonished.

Satisfied, my mother jumped off and strode beside the wagon. I hugged Lothar, and he clung to me.

Ever since then, I have had a passion for protecting little ones. It still moves me to tears when I think about children who are caught in the throes of war. Children do not understand what is taking place around them, but they suffer the most. There is no greater evil on this planet than war! Even so, come Lord Jesus, and put an end to all of the chaos and suffering!

I have to pull myself together as I tell my story because I often cry recalling the memories and emotions from that time. Above all, I can say that the Lord is good. He protected us, and He helped us. I have considered what the experience must have been like for my mother, and I forgave her a long time ago. After all, she was just trying to raise three little children and bring them through the terrors of war with no support, and without her husband. It was a fight for survival.

## THE RUSSIANS IN PURSUIT

We had made a trek of one thousand kilometers (over six hundred miles) before it was all over. It was a marathon for survival: walking, running, crossing bridges just before they blew up, always with the Russian army in close pursuit. We were not privy to know what lay ahead or where we would spend the next day or night. Two German soldiers accompanied us on our journey, and they drove us like cattle, making sure the required distance was covered every day from one town to the next. We slept wherever we found shelter.

On the first night, I was filled with guilt, thinking about how I'd longed for something new and exciting. I felt responsible for our predicament because I had prayed for adventure. I spent that night crammed into a large iron bed with four other kids. Sleep eluded me. Other nights we slept in churches, where the pews had been pushed to the sides to make room for us on cold, hard floors. Some nights we slept in schools, where straw and hay had been strewn on the floors. We slept wherever there was room for all of us to sleep.

## OMINOUS ENCOUNTER IN A TRAIN STATION

Sometimes I couldn't sleep, especially after an encounter at a train station during our escape from the Russians. We were not boarding a train, but for some reason our group stopped at the station. As we stood near the tracks, a cattle train pulled in. But it was not filled with cattle; it was filled with people. We heard voices crying out and begging for water. We saw hands thrust between the slats, pleading for help.

We found out that the train was filled with Jews. This is the only time I was aware that something dreadful was happening to the Jews. If my parents knew about it, they didn't share it with us.

As we stood there listening to them cry for help, my mother, aunt, and other adults began yelling at the German soldiers: "Give them water! Give them some water!" But the soldiers remained motionless, without expression. So, my mother and my aunt grabbed their handbags and began hitting the soldiers, shouting, "Do something! Give them water!"

The train began to move, pulling out of the station. Away it went, along with the pleading cries of the suffering ones.

The whole event was traumatic for me. It was an encounter that could not be excused or explained in any way, and to this day it haunts me.

## BAD SOUP, ROTTEN BOLOGNA

A common meal during that time was watery soup and a piece of bread. It was all that was available to feed a large group of people. Sometimes the food available was not fit to eat. One day, when we were served pea soup, we saw little worms floating on the top. I was fortunate that, being so small, I didn't need much to eat. As it was, I could barely stomach the food I was given. One day my mother and aunt must have figured the bologna being handed out was not edible. They knew we were hungry, but they forbade us to eat it. Their judgment proved correct. The lunch meat was rotten, and everybody who ate it got diarrhea. Intestinal parasites (worms) were a reality of our daily lives. What a mess that was with no bathrooms nearby!

## MAKESHIFT OUTHOUSE

I cannot fathom how mothers endure watching their children suffer in these circumstances. There were no accommodations for keeping clean on the road. Sometimes we found a stream or lake, but there was no place to take a proper bath or shower. There were no provisions for toilet or hygiene.

I recall arriving in one town that had prepared for a slew of wagons and refugees. The townspeople had dug a big trench and put barrels with wooden planks across it as makeshift outhouses. The outhouses were patrolled by guards to keep peace and order, but I felt neither peace nor order and could not make myself use these facilities. I waited to find bushes to hide behind, to do my business. I cannot seem to remember what we used for toilet paper; it may well have been old newspapers. Whenever I see huge masses of refugees on TV news, the memories rush back—I know what it is like. It is hard to convey the full impact; you really had to be there to understand how it felt. Of course, it's not an experience I wish for anyone!

## LICE

Because of the harsh, unsanitary conditions, I was covered in sores, scabs, and lice. My mother combatted the wily critters with her lice comb. She told me to hold my head over a sheet of newspaper while she combed the lice out of my hair. I can still remember that awful "click, click" sound the lice made as they fell onto the paper. I'll never understand why my mother kept my hair long when it would have been more practical to cut it short. Of course, I had no say in the matter.

## THE GOOD WITH THE BAD

Our plight as refugees included good and bad experiences. We lived in a state of ignorance, never knowing what awaited us at the next destination. One town in Czechoslovakia holds two poignant memories for me, one dreadful and the other miraculous.

We had just arrived in the town where we were supposed to spend the night. We children waited together on the snowy street, as our mothers went to inquire about sleeping accommodations. A local boy signaled us from across the street. He held a big, long stick and waved it at us. We thought he was asking us to play. Without hesitating or examining the stick, I ran to him and grabbed the end he offered. It didn't take long to realize my mistake. The boy was not making a gesture of goodwill. He had swirled the stick through human waste, and excrement covered my hand!

Phew! I flung the stick away and grabbed a handful of snow to clean off my hand. What struck me deeply was not the fact that I had touched the filthy thing, but how even children can turn against each other during war. To me, war is of the Devil, and I am so thankful that the Word of God tells us that when Jesus comes back, war will cease forever. I cannot think of anything more devastating than war, especially for the little ones.

The terrible memory of that day was almost canceled by a sort of miracle when my family experienced a beautiful act of kindness by a woman who lived in that town. She was outside her home when she noticed how exhausted and filthy we refugees were. She motioned for us to come inside. She spoke Czech, and my mother spoke German, but even though there was a language barrier, they were able to communicate when they made the sign of the cross and realized they were both Christians.

We had been on the road for a few weeks and hadn't slept in a proper bed, but that night we were able to take a hot bath and sleep in a real bed with clean sheets. I will never forget the feeling of utter bliss! The future dream of "clean sheets, fresh flowers, and a horse" was birthed in me at that time.

The next morning, when it was time to continue our journey, I saw my mother and this woman embracing and crying. On the one hand, we experienced hatred, animosity, and violence, and on the other hand, thanks to our Lord Jesus, we experienced love and compassion through the generosity of this Christian woman.

## LOW-FLYING AIRPLANES

We had to be prepared at all times for low-flying airplanes. Though it is no longer considered acceptable, during World War II, the Allies would actually target civilians and try to kill as many as possible, whether by dropping bombs in towns or over open fields. The German guards trained us to drop to the ground and lie flat, seek shelter, or even hide in the trees. On one occasion, even though it was already May, an enormous snow cloud overshadowed our entire caravan of refugees, protecting us from aerial attacks.

I am certain that we were in constant, deadly danger, but the Lord saw us through and preserved our lives. Many around us were shot or died from other causes, but by His mercy, we survived—my mother, brothers, aunt, cousins, and I.

## WOMEN LED THE JOURNEY

It was fortunate that my mother was a natural-born leader. Because many husbands and fathers were at war, the only males accompanying us on our journey were old and frail, or very young. Hitler had drafted not only men but male youth—anyone who could hold his own. As a result, the responsibility to lead fell to the women, and my mother would often be the one to take charge.

One way my mother took the lead was by scouting out the next town on a bicycle, pedaling ahead of the wagon train to ensure we would be safe there. I am not certain I would have been able to leave my children behind if I had been in her place. I cannot imagine the anguish my mother felt as she pedaled ahead, away from her children toward danger. But someone had to do it. We were warned regularly that the next town could be occupied by the enemy. While a military presence had accompanied us at the start of our trek, the two soldiers had been called to the war front, abandoning us to our own resources. The threat of the raping, plundering, murdering Russians drove us on, and my mother scouted ahead. I shall always be grateful for her stalwart courage.

## NEVER-ENDING HUNGER

Fear drove us on, and hunger was our constant companion. One day it was so bitterly cold, my mother put some cooked potatoes in her coat pockets to keep warm, but the subzero temperatures cut through the fabric and froze them solid. Sometimes my mother and aunt would attempt to unearth a few edible plants in fields on the side of the road. Once they found some leftover sweet potatoes.

We were glad to find food, but because we had to eat them raw, they tasted horrible. To this day, I do not like sweet potatoes or yams.

## WHO BURIED THE DEAD?

An old man was traveling on one of the wagons. He always sat at the very back, near the wheel axles. A few weeks later, we noticed he wasn't there anymore. We were told he had frozen to death and fallen off the wagon. There was no question of taking his body with us, and he had been left behind. *We wondered who, if anyone, buried the old man.*

Another traveler, a woman, walked alone pushing a baby carriage with a newborn baby inside, while a small child walked by her side. The baby in the carriage froze to death. *We wondered who, if anyone, buried the baby.*

Another time, we found refuge in a barn alongside pigs and other animals. That night a woman in our group went into labor. Nobody seemed to know how to help her, and there was certainly no doctor. Consequently, she and her baby died trying to deliver.

Once again, little ones suffered, especially the woman's children, who needed someone to care for them. *We wondered who, if anyone, buried the mother and baby.*

## A FRIENDLY BEAST

Sometime later we spent a night in a horse barn. I was afraid of horses, but there was no place else to stay. We slept separated from the horses by a five-foot wall. During the night, I was awakened by a loud noise. I jumped up off the straw and bumped my head. When I turned to see what I had hit, I was surprised to find a horse peering over the wall, watching me. I had bumped into him! I almost screamed, but the horse's nose was soft, and he made soft neighing noises. I stood on tiptoes and stroked his head and mane. I felt so comforted by his gentleness.

While I was petting the gentle creature, I realized I had not been awakened by the horse, but by a thunderstorm raging outside. I had always been afraid of thunder and lightning, but I wasn't afraid anymore. That night I was not only delivered from my fear of horses but of thunder and lightning as well. These fears paled in comparison to the death and hunger we faced daily in our fight for survival.

## TREACHEROUS PASSAGE

As I mentioned before, our route was mapped through Czechoslovakia across the Eulengebirge mountain range to our destination in Czechoslovakia. As we made our way deeper into the heart of the mountains, we followed a precarious path with steep cliffs to our left. We children watched several cows slip and fall, their legs split apart on the icy road as they tumbled over the cliffs to their death. As you would expect, we traveled very slowly with great trepidation and caution, all the while surrounded by snow and ice, with the enemy behind us.

Our journey seemed hopeless, and I would learn much later that at one point my aunt was so distraught she wanted to give up and end it all by drowning her children and herself in a lake we were passing. Once again, my mother, the strong one, prevented this tragedy from happening, reasoning with my aunt and appealing to her conscience.

## GERMANY SURRENDERS

At last, the war was winding down, and our wagon train finally disbanded. My family found refuge with some Czech farmers who offered their garage as a temporary dwelling. By now, there were far fewer travelers than when we started. How many perished on our journey, God only knows, but it must have been hundreds.

Even though we had a place to stay, each day brought the challenge of survival. For the entire year that we were in Czechoslovakia, "enemy territory," contact with former friends and family was lost. We were on our own.

While we lived in the garage, news reached us that Germany had unconditionally surrendered. It was May 8, 1945, and "Uncle Hitler" was dead. My mother cried, but we children did not understand why. To this day, I still do not really know why she was troubled by the loss of this evil dictator. But fear of being left alone, with three little ones to care for in enemy territory, must have overwhelmed her. Perhaps her tears were in knowing that the place she called "home" was lost forever.

In any case, it was the end of one horrific era and the beginning of a time of more suffering.

## A SURGE OF EVIL BEFORE SURRENDER

The few weeks before Germany's surrender, there was an upsurge of evil. Satan knew that the war was ending, and violent acts of murder and sexual crimes seemed to be more rampant than ever. Two women from our trek, one of whom was mentally handicapped, were raped and suffered the effects of shock and lasting psychological scars. Both became pregnant by their assailants and would give birth to their babies in Tachau, Czechoslovakia, at the refugee camp to which we would be assigned.

## SCHOOLING CONTINUES IN WAR

I still find it strange that during the short time we lived in that garage, we had to attend school. Germans were fanatics when it came to schooling and education. I remember how Fred and I had to walk a substantial distance in order to get to an old schoolhouse. It still amazes me that parents would insist upon sending their children to school under such grim circumstances.

That schoolhouse sat high upon a hill. As we walked, we listened for the ever-dreaded, low-flying airplanes. If we heard one, we were to duck, lie flat on the ground, and wait until it passed. The fact that this was still necessary made it evident that the war was not really over. One day on our way to school, we heard the sound of an airplane coming closer. Immediately, we sought shelter in a large cement irrigation pipe. Fred and I crawled in from opposite ends and waited until the danger passed. While we hunkered there, we noticed a small rabbit trapped in the pipe and scampering to and fro between us, trying to escape. After the airplane left, Fred and I crawled out, followed by Peter Cottontail, happy to be free. It is odd, the things you remember from the strangest times!

School wasn't always book learning. One day at that schoolhouse on the hill, we witnessed an outrageous act of aggression. A train rumbled through the valley. I wished I could wave to the conductor, but from our vantage point on the hill, the conductor and the train looked like tiny toys. A low-flying airplane circled above the train. We saw a machine gun on the plane, and we saw the machine gunner shoot the conductor, causing the train to derail right in front of our eyes!

In retrospect, I am astounded at how tough I was, how tough all the children were to survive those terrible times. Of course, if we children hadn't been so resilient, generations would have been wiped out, and I wouldn't be here telling my story!

## 4,000,000 WOMEN AND CHILDREN PERISH

I want to emphasize how the destiny of our family was covered by the Lord's mercy. I don't know if it is well-known, but four-million, not four-hundred-thousand, but 4,000,000 German women and children perished in Germany due to the acts of World War II. Many lost their lives as a result of Allied bombings. After we left Stettin, we were fortunate to escape the bombings that demolished countless large towns. Thousands upon thousands died in those raids, and others died on long winter treks and wagon trains such as I have just described. Still, others died from illness and disease. It is nothing short of a miracle that any of us survived these horrors!

## REFUGEE CAMP

The war was over, and Germany was defeated. Everywhere we turned there was utter chaos—huge numbers of refugees, like ourselves, filled the streets of Czechoslovakia, and no one knew what to do with us.

In June 1945, the Czechs brought us to an evacuated concentration camp in Tachau, Czechoslovakia, where Jews, other prisoners, and opponents of the Third Reich had been held during Hitler's rule. We lived there for about a year. We had to wear white armbands at all times, identifying us as Germans. The barracks were equipped with triple bunk beds, and each barrack held about forty to fifty people. In the center of each barrack were one wooden table with benches and a wood stove; that was the extent of the furnishings.

# OUTHOUSE HORRORS

We spent one year in the refugee camp, and what I remember most is the lack of hygiene. We had to use an outhouse on a hill away from the barracks. The outhouse was a little shed with two entrances, one for women and girls and one for men and boys. But both sides were connected, and it was easy to reach underneath the wall to the other side.

As I sat there one day, somebody from the other side—some boy—stretched his hand under the wall and grabbed me. I was scared and repulsed!

That year, from 1945 to 1946, we encountered another dreadfully cold winter. Everything was frozen, including the hill that led up to the outhouse. Several times we had to crawl on our hands and knees to get there.

One day, when the ice melted and the ground thawed, the septic tank needed to be drained. With four to five hundred refugees living at that camp, it had filled up quickly. While the adults were emptying the huge hole, a small boy fell into it. The adults tried to pull him out with a long staff, but he couldn't hold on. The stick slipped out of his grasp and down he went again. It was a horrible sight!

Another attempt was successful, and he was rescued. But for days afterward, I relived the event in my mind and wondered what it must have been like for that little boy—which left me nauseous and sick to my stomach. I had an extremely vivid imagination, as well as an empathetic soul, and it was easy for me to put myself in his place and experience what he must have suffered.

# MY OWN MIRACLE

The food shortage was awful the first few months before the Americans arrived. Many people threw caution to the wind and ate whatever they could scavenge. They were so starved, they ignored the bugs or worms we often discovered in the food, and they devoured whatever rations they were given. As a child, I remember how the clothes hung loosely on other children and the adults. If I had caught a glimpse of myself in a mirror, I'm sure I reflected the same image. The only blessing in this was that no mirrors were to be had.

Once again, I was happy to be small. I didn't need much and wasn't able to stomach much that was available. But others had to eat, and we were constantly on the hunt for something—anything—to eat. We children would spend our free time looking for stinging nettles that could be cooked and tasted like spinach. We had to be careful gathering nettles because they could irritate our skin if we touched them the wrong way.

The Czechs imposed a curfew, set for dusk. Rightly so, because danger lurked in the streets, particularly for Germans. After the fall of Hitler and the Nazi regime, many neighboring countries, including the Czechs, wanted revenge. We were instructed not to leave the fenced-in camp where our barracks were. But children being children, we made holes in the fences and snuck out anyway. We knew there was a greater chance to find something edible in the fields outside.

One day, I left the barracks with a group of children, to look for food. Being a dreamer and drawn to beautiful things, I got distracted. A patch of wildflowers captured my attention, and I wandered over to them, separating myself from the rest of the group. While the other kids searched for nettles, I picked flowers, cascading away in a wanderlust.

All of a sudden, I heard yelling. It was not the friendly shouting of my friends; it was serious shouting in a language I didn't know. I thought it was Czech. I looked up and saw a group of teenage boys wielding branches the size of baseball bats. To a little girl, they looked like giants. The children I had come with observed the boys and then ran back to camp. But my escape was blocked; blocked by a wall of vicious, jeering teenagers, hatred seething from their eyes. I was trapped!

The boys approached me, continuing to yell. Fear rising and my heart pounding; how would I escape? I ran as fast as my little legs could carry me, the bullies hot on my trail.

Suddenly I found myself in front of a house, pounding

frantically on the front door. What happened next was like a dream. A kind woman appeared before me and, though she spoke no German, she must have seen the utter terror and desperation in my eyes. She immediately took me to her backyard and hid me in a chicken coop. I cowered there, trembling, waiting, and listening as the woman sent the boys away. I could hear faintly their language being spoken between this kind woman and the teenagers, though I couldn't understand what was being spoken. After a while, the woman gestured for me to come out, gave me a pat on the back, and sent me back to camp.

I ran like never before, all the way back to the camp. Later, looking back, I felt as though I had experienced the story recorded in Acts 8:39, where Philip encounters the Ethiopian in the desert, because a little short-legged girl *cannot* outrun a mob of big teenagers! Like Phillip, I had been transported over a distance, and the Spirit had saved me from whatever torment those boys had planned for me.

When I returned to camp, my mother gave me a good whipping. I suppose I deserved it—but the whole experience was miraculous to me. How merciful was the Lord to this little one!

## RATION STAMPS BUT NO SALT

After the American soldiers had arrived, things in camp began to improve little by little. We were given food stamps and allowed to go into town to buy provisions—mostly bread. Some townspeople showed us kindness, like the woman who worked at a local grocery store. I believe she was a Christian.

We were only allowed a certain ration of stamps per day. But my brother Fred would return to the store more frequently than we were supposed to. He would dress in different clothes or wear a hat in hopes of disguising himself and getting a little more food that day. This kind shopkeeper would pretend not to recognize him and let him buy more bread. We had suffered hunger for such a long time, even a little bread felt like Christmas!

We experienced a shortage of many things, one of them salt. We would have gladly given multiple portions of sugar for just one portion of salt. The food that was available to eat was terrible, and without salt, it was even worse.

One of the basic human tastes, salt is essential for life. Human tissue contains larger quantities of salt than do plants. One of the oldest food seasonings known to man, salt has also been used throughout time for food preservation. It's no wonder that the scarcity and universal need for salt has led nations to go to war over it. It would be months before we would savor salt on our tongues.

This experience teaches me the importance of our Lord's warning that "if the salt has lost its savor, it is good for nothing but to be trodden under foot of men." This concerns all believers who are not living in truth.

## SCHOOL CONTINUES

As always, children who were seven or older were required to attend school. As long as it wasn't raining, our classes took place under a tree in a field. I don't remember what I actually learned during that time, but I took a liking to anything that involved making things beautiful. I loved to cut paper to make little doilies. I loved to pick wildflowers, arrange them in empty tin cans, and put them around our barracks to beautify the bleak surroundings. To this day, flowers are a passion of mine.

## BITTERSWEET BIRTHS

I related earlier that two women in our trek were due to give birth, and it was now their time. Our excitement to welcome the little ones was bittersweet. Their babies had been conceived as a result of rape in the surge that preceded Germany's surrender. Both women were taken away from the barracks to deliver their babies. We heard that someone tried to take the handicapped woman's child, even though she was insistent upon keeping it. We never learned the fate of these mothers and their little ones. I can only imagine how devastating it must have been for them.

## NIGHT TERRORS

Frequently, throughout the night, our barrack was awakened by a young boy with severe nightmares—a condition known today as night terrors. The boy would scream very loudly for long periods of time. It was necessary to shake him in order to wake him from his terror. This was a very frightening experience for the rest of us children, which caused us great anxiety.

## MIRACLES AND NEIGHBORLY KINDNESS

In His mercy, the Lord intervened as little miracles continued to occur in our lives. The Red Cross, along with the American soldiers, offered assistance to my mother and aunt, helping us get in touch with our relatives in Detroit, Michigan. These included my mother's three brothers and sister who had immigrated to the United States in 1933, a few years prior to the start of the war. They began sending us packages of food, clothing, and other supplies we desperately needed.

Excitement was in the air whenever a package arrived. The whole barrack felt it, knowing that we would share what we had received, just as others would share their gifts with us. I saw this neighborly kindness manifest itself time after time. Once the war was over, and we were no longer in imminent danger of losing our lives, we got beyond survival mentality and looked out for each other. I learned the importance of sharing and how much joy it brought to everyone.

## MY MOTHER, THE DRESSMAKER

As I have said, my mother was an excellent seamstress. One day she got hold of some burlap bags and carefully hand-tailored a dress for me, detailing it with embroidery. She was very proud of that dress, but sadly, I couldn't wear it. My skin was very sensitive, and the rough material was so abrasive, it made me cry. My skin required softer fabric, like worn, hand-me-down rags, and that's what I wore: cotton frocks tailored from my mother's or aunt's old dresses, or garments donated by charities like the Red Cross, the Salvation Army, or CARE. I was seventeen before I owned a store-bought dress, purchased with my own money!

## AMERICAN SOLDIERS AND CHEWING GUM

We sure did love the American soldiers! They gave us candy and introduced us to chewing gum. But, before they gave us the gum or candy, they had their fun with us. They'd line us up in a row and tell us to shout, "Heil, Hitler!" We wanted the treats so we clapped our heels together and saluted them with our hands held high, imitating the customary salutation during "Uncle Hitler's" reign. The soldiers had a good laugh and rewarded us with candy and gum.

When my mother found out about the candy, chocolate, or chewing gum we had received, she was curious to know where it came from. We told her about the soldiers and what we had done. She and my aunt were horrified and forbade us to ever do it again. We didn't keep our promise and most certainly did it again, and we were rewarded with more candy and gum. We just made sure our mothers didn't find out.

It would only be much later that we would come to understand that it was because of "Uncle Hitler" that we were in these circumstances in the first place!

## MUSIC IN OUR CAMP

My mother and Aunt Hille were both skilled guitar players, and they told us stories about singing with the American soldiers in the evenings. "You Are My Sunshine" was one of the songs they learned. My mother and aunt admitted, as well, the ever-present temptation to flirt with the soldiers; after all, they were both young and their husbands had been gone for two years. The women received many "offers," but they both remained pure and faithful to their marriages. There was, however, one girl in our camp, a teenager, who succumbed to the advances of one of the Americans, and she got pregnant. When the soldiers were sent home, the young mother was left to care for her infant alone. She raised him well, but not without many challenges and much suffering. We never lost contact with her family, and we know the child grew up to be a fine young man. I always thought it was too bad he never knew his father.

## MY MOTHER LETS DOWN HER GUARD

Many people bury their memories so they don't have to deal with the pain. For whatever reason, my mother buried hers. I was hard-pressed to get any stories from her. She was not one who shared easily. However, one night was different. It was many years after the war, in 1987, and I was visiting my family in Germany. I felt there were things Mother and I needed to talk about, and I pressed for discussion. I was pleasantly surprised when we stayed up until the wee hours sharing memories.

That was when my mother revealed this devastating story. It happened during our trek, escaping the Russians. We children must have been napping at the time our wagon train stopped. My mother said she saw many sick and dying German civilians huddled on the side of the road. Some of them lay stretched out on torn bales of hay, like bodies in the morgue. They cried out to her and begged her to read Scripture to them. She was a believer and always carried a small Bible with her. She told me it was Psalm 91 that carried her through the war years. She obliged the sick and dying Germans, reading to them and praying with them. That was all she could do before she got the order that the wagon train would move on. *We wondered who, if anyone, would bury all the dead.*

The morning after she told me this story, she said she had not slept a wink. She had not been able to put her mind to rest all night, and she would never ever talk about those times again. "After all," she added, "it is of no use to remember or discuss these things." In her mind, what was done was done.

I, on the other hand, think it's important to share these memories, to pass them on, to learn to become better people, to be kind to each other.

## DECISION TIME: EAST OR WEST

In June 1946, our refugee camp in Czechoslovakia was disbanded, and it was time to move on again. At this point, we experienced another miraculous intervention. By that time, Germany had been divided into East and West. The directive was for refugees from the west to be placed on a train to West Germany, and refugees from the east to be placed on a train back to East Germany. We had come from Stettin, which had been in East Germany but had been returned to Poland. My mother and aunt were terrified at the thought of returning to that place, but according to the directive, we had no right to go west. In the struggle to survive, most people had lost all of their belongings, including their identification papers, which made it difficult to prove which trains they should board. But, my mother kept our papers in her ever-present, *big, black handbag*.

The decisive moment came when my mother, our spokesperson, would have to answer to the authorities. To take the train to the east or to take the train to the west—that was the question. My mother and my aunt knew that some way, somehow, we had to make it to the west. She was afraid that if she said we were eligible to go to the west, they would know she was not telling the truth, and we would be found out. She wasn't good at lying, and she didn't want to lie, but she didn't want to go east either.

Shaking and trembling, we stood in line in the outdoor marketplace with our mothers, waiting our turn to face the authorities. Moments before we reached the front of the line, a commotion broke out on the other side of the market. Everyone stretched and strained to see and hear what was happening, and the American soldiers made their way toward the upheaval to maintain peace. It turned out that an old, frail man was suffering a heart attack. We had all been standing outside in the summer's heat for quite some time, and it must have been too much for him to bear. He died that day.

But, in the midst of the confusion and tumult, my mother and my aunt gave each other one quick look, grabbed us children, and made a beeline for the westbound train. That is how we made it to West Germany!

I think it was a miraculous intervention, and we were eternally grateful! We likened it to the sacrificial death of the Lord Jesus Christ so that we could live forever. I also believe that during those times, many an American soldier chose to look the other way. God bless them for it!

## THREE DAYS ON A CATTLE TRAIN

We spent three long days on the train, which had originally been for cattle. We, like those unfortunate beasts, were crammed into tight quarters with dozens of others, empty-handed except for what we could carry on our persons.

The floor of the cattle car was covered in hay, and there was a small bucket in the corner that served as a toilet, which would be emptied from time to time. Our train made its way slowly past vast landscapes and through towns that had been utterly devastated by the war. We had no water to wash ourselves, only a little to drink, and small pieces of bread to eat. Our clothes were soiled with dust and dirt and sweat, and the stench was nauseating.

But, we were free!

## ARM BANDS REMOVED

When we crossed the border from Czechoslovakia into Germany, the entire train erupted with shouts of joy. As German refugees, we had been forced to wear white arm bands—but now that we were safely on German soil, we could remove them.

Great excitement ensued, as people threw their arm bands

out of the train. There were so many arm bands lying on the ground, it looked like a snowstorm had blanketed the shoulders of the tracks!

The train kept moving forward, closer to home by the mile, but we still didn't know what the next day would bring, what to expect, or where we would end up.

## MY AUNT AND COUSINS LEAVE US

As soon as we returned to Germany, Aunt Hille and her two daughters, Ute and Adelheid, left us and went to a town near Hannover, where they had relatives. We bade one another a tearful and heartfelt farewell and parted ways. The sense of loss was great—we had experienced and survived so much together, seen horrors and miracles, and even preserved my aunt's life when she felt unable to bear any more.

Following this chaotic season of our life, my cousin, Ute, developed a pathological fear of going hungry. To this day, she is determined to have the best-stocked pantry and freezer you could imagine. She has a beautiful garden and cans large quantities of fruit and vegetables. It never occurred to me to fear going hungry, probably because I was much smaller and not so dependent on food.

At that point, we didn't know where my father was, or whether he was alive or dead. If he had survived, we did not know whether he would be able to find us. Try as we might, we were unable to locate him. The pain of this was nearly unbearable.

## NEXT STOP BAVARIA

In June 1946, we arrived in Neustadt bei Coburg, Bavaria, a few kilometers from the border with East Germany and about fifteen kilometers from the city of Coburg. What were we to do now? We looked around, and everything was in ruins. Rebuilding had yet to take place, and all of Germany was in a state of chaos.

As the solution seemed to be all too often, we were once again placed in a refugee camp. This time, we were housed in an evacuated prisoner of war camp on the outskirts of Neustadt.

On my first trip into town with my mother, I was struck by the way the people talked. Their language sounded foreign, and I could hardly understand what they were saying. I was confused and asked my mother, "Are you sure we are in Germany?" Every region in Germany has a different dialect, but this one was so different from the High German I was accustomed to that I was sincerely under the impression we must be in another country.

But we were the ones who were different, and the locals were not afraid to show us their disdain. They looked down on us as the "ragged refugees." So began yet another period in which we would feel alienated, persecuted, and unwanted—even on our native soil. The war was over, but it still raged in people's hearts, and there was still a lot of fear and hatred to overcome. We were labeled *Fremma*, which loosely translated means foreigner, stranger, or refugee. We were marked not only by our extreme poverty but by the way we talked.

Language differences have always been my challenge, and I have always stood out as different. I never did learn a German dialect and stuck to my roots of High German. That was all I knew, but I was aware that to some Germans, I sounded arrogant and aloof. Currently, I live in America, where English is spoken, and my German accent tells everyone I'm from somewhere else. But since I speak English well, we understand each other, and no one thinks I'm snooty … just different!

## SHARING THE BARRACKS

This camp near Neustadt would be our home for a year. It was comprised of barracks, each one holding three families whose living quarters were separated by blankets strung over clotheslines. Even though we had our own space, we were aware of the happenings in the other families. Privacy was nonexistent. My mother said that in some ways this part of our journey to survive was worse than the actual war because we were forced to live with "lowlife, crude, filthy people" who did not value hygiene or cleanliness.

One example of this lack of care and cleanliness was in the way our housemates kept the common areas. We were provided an outdoor chemical toilet, along with small potties for the children. There was a long wash basin for everyone to wash their dishes and to use for running water and cleaning. But, rather than disposing of their potty waste into the toilet, these lazy, slothful families would dump their human waste into the common wash basin. My mother was so horrified she began to pray that these people would leave. And they did! We were soon blessed with new housemates in our barrack who were decent and made living together more manageable.

## BATTLING BEDBUGS

The old barracks boasted a nonhuman challenge: bedbugs. When these pests became too much to bear, the management that oversaw our camp ordered everyone out of their barracks and into the main house for two nights, during which time they would try to rid the infested buildings of the bugs.

The main house wasn't much better; it was in abominable condition and had only a few mattresses in each room. There was hardly anyplace to walk or do much other than lie down to sleep. While we suffered the pitfalls of the main house, attempts to rid the bedbugs were underway.

Containers with a mud-like filling were placed around the barracks and lit on fire, filling the barracks with a horrible stench that lingered for weeks after we had moved back in. But it was all for naught. Before long the bedbugs would be back, and the whole process would begin again.

## MY FATHER'S WAR

As all of us fought to survive during these long years, Father likewise had his own journey to endure. We did not know what was transpiring in his life, but we would later learn about some of the challenges he overcame.

After the last bombing in Stettin in 1943, the one that forced us to evacuate our home and our town, my father was drafted into the army. As I related earlier, because he had suffered tuberculosis and still bore a scar on his lungs, he was restricted to serving at a desk job. When desk jobs became scarce, he was assigned to guard prisoners of war, and those prisoners were Americans.

A gregarious man, Father made friends with many of these soldiers who were considered our enemies. If the German soldiers had known about my father's kindness toward the American soldiers, it would have cost him dearly.

He told us how he once got into a very sticky situation. One day, in the company of the prisoners, he set his gun down in order to play checkers with them. One of his superiors caught him without his weapon and threatened to take him to court and charge him with fraternization with the enemy if it ever happened again. My father knew he could have been shot as punishment for his behavior.

According to my father, the German army knew the war was coming to an end days before the unconditional surrender on May 8, 1945. Once the surrender took place, many of the superiors chose not to show their faces in public anymore.

At that point, my father decided he was going to let all of his prisoners go free. He said it was almost comical to see soldiers and prisoners fraternizing, walking to and fro, slapping palms in jubilation, wishing each other a fond farewell, and heading for freedom—most certainly toward the West.

After the surrender, my father embarked upon his own journey, trying to make his way home on foot, walking from Mecklenburg to Glauchau, which was now in East Germany. He hoped to find his mother or other relatives who might be able to assist him. He spent his nights anywhere he could, often in a stable or a barn. Some farmers working in the fields offered him old clothes to replace his uniform, and food to stay alive. Twice he was captured by American soldiers, but he was not afraid. They paid very little attention to him, so he escaped both times.

There was another army, however, that captured him and held him firmly in captivity. The Russian military had advanced toward the West, and my father fell into their grasp. He was forced to live in a camp and do hard physical labor, repairing and rebuilding a railroad. He suffered excruciating hunger, eating anything, even grass, just to subsist. Still, the Lord was with him.

In May 1946, my father somehow managed to escape by climbing over the huge fence surrounding the camp. When I heard his story, I had to smile. I couldn't picture my father scaling a fence because he had never been athletic or strong. But I gave him credit for determination.

With his last piece of bread, my father bribed a border guard to allow him entrance from East Germany into West Germany. At that time everything was in a state of disarray, and there were no fences, barbed wire, or guard dogs. He made it easily across the border, where he found assistance through the Red Cross and was informed of our whereabouts in Bavaria. He wasted no time walking hundreds of miles to find us. My father was stronger than I ever knew!

## WOLLIN FAMILY REUNITED

The day finally came in June 1946, when the Wollin family was reunited in the camp near Neustadt, Bavaria. The Hand of the Lord was upon us and had worked in great provision for our family. We had survived. That alone was miraculous!

Furthermore, although the majority of Berlin had been leveled to the ground, some buildings had remained intact. Hard as it is to believe, one of these buildings contained archived files, and important papers had been preserved, including papers that verified my father's employment history. He went on to work as a bookkeeper for Siemens, was promoted, and after thirty-one faithful years of service, my father received a generous retirement pension.

Father loved the United States because of generous American Quakers who had assisted him when he was a child. He had been a hungry little boy when World War I ended. Some Quakers from America arranged a feeding program for German school children, and without their help, my father might not have survived. That's when his high regard for the United States began, and he had always wanted to live there.

But his immigration to the U.S. was not to be. Because of his bout with tuberculosis, from which he had recovered, he was not permitted to enter. Not even the letter from General Love, the prisoner he had befriended, helped.

We all shared his disappointment, but I came to see his rejection as God's foresight. I believe the Lord was looking out for my father's security. After all, Father was not a man's man; he was not especially strong, nor was he skilled at working with his hands. He might have struggled to make a living to provide for our family in America, and he might have encountered animosity from Americans who considered Germans their enemies.

So, the Lord was in control, guiding us even in these circumstances. Whatever evil the enemy threw at us, God turned it into good. Much later, my father was able to visit the country he loved fifteen times, including California and other places, and when he returned to Germany, he hosted slide shows and wrote freelance articles for two local newspapers, always singing the praises of his beloved United States of America. By this time, the realization of the atrocities committed by the Germans against Jews and others had become common knowledge, exposed in the newspapers and schools. Father's lectures were well received in his homeland.

## DESPERATE FOR FOOD

The family was now reunited, but food in the camp near Neustadt bei Coburg was still hard to find. Hygiene, however, had improved after our crude housemates moved out, and we had running water, though it was ice cold. We also had a small wood stove on which to heat water and an area where we could to wash. But as far as food provision, our situation was dire, as it was throughout all of Germany. I don't know if we would have survived without the support of our relatives in the United States.

Sometimes, at the point of desperation, a package would arrive, and we would have just enough to get us through the next few days. The package would contain food, of course, but also luxuries like coffee, cigarettes, and clothing, which was used to barter for food from surrounding farmers.

Once during the winter, on an exceptionally cold day, our family made its way treacherously on foot from one farmhouse to the next. We had received some warm underwear from America and hoped to be able to exchange it for potatoes or bread. But no one wanted the underwear. With heavy hearts and rumbling stomachs, we trudged back to the camp. Our cupboards were empty. But when we returned, we received a package from Detroit! The Lord sustained us over and over again.

## A SPECIAL CHRISTMAS

Christmas of the year my father returned was very special, partly because of the aid we received from America. It is a German tradition for children to attend a church service on Christmas Eve while their parents decorate the Christmas tree and put presents underneath. As soon as the children return home, they bide their time in a darkened room to wait until the candles on the tree are lit, and the room is aglow with soft, warm light. The magic of real candles on a tree is so delightful and to little children, like stars dancing on the branches. This German Christmas tradition is still being practiced by some today, a custom that can't be duplicated by modern electric lights.

In keeping with tradition, my two brothers and I walked through the snow for two kilometers, along with some of the other children from our camp, to attend the Christmas Eve service at a local church. As we made our way back to our barrack, we did not expect to have a Christmas tree, receive presents, or enjoy a bountiful feast. We knew our circumstances were dire. But to our great surprise, the minute we stepped inside we saw a sweet little tree on the long wooden table with several gifts placed beneath. The fragrance of that freshly cut tree from the local forest permeated the air. We were delighted beyond belief!

I was speechless, though only for a moment. One of the presents brought me great joy: a baby doll! Something I had desperately wanted, but after the Barbie-like doll incident never dared to ask. We also received sweets and all the food we could eat. What a Christmas it had turned out to be!

We asked our parents how this miraculous celebration came to be. In those days, parents wanted their children to believe that *Christkind* (the Christ Child) brought the presents, not Santa Claus. But our parents told us the true story. Our relatives in Detroit had sent a large quantity of much-coveted coffee and cigarettes. My parents were never smokers, so they were able to use the cigarettes to barter or sell, which, in turn, allowed them to purchase all the wonderful food and gifts for us.

But I believe there was another truth to the story. I believe our gracious and compassionate Lord Jesus was guiding my parents that Christmas. Getting gifts and candy doesn't sound very spiritual, but I believe the Lord sees the longings of every little heart and takes great delight in fulfilling their secret desires. Many meager Christmas celebrations followed, but that year's feast was so special and so miraculous, it stays in my memory as though it happened yesterday.

Sometimes the little ones move so fast, it seems even the Lord Jesus can't catch them in time, and that's what happened that Christmas. My little brother Lothar was so thrilled with every toy he received, he couldn't contain his joy. He was anxious to run outside and show everyone his presents, but his feet moved faster than his brain. When he leaped off the steps of the barrack, he slipped on the ice, fell head over heels, and broke his leg—for the second time. Poor little guy! Lothar had more accidents in his younger days than the rest of us children put together.

# LIFE GOES ON AND SO DOES SCHOOL

Lothar recovered, and the happy holidays were followed by school, always school. The winter mornings were icy, and we had to walk a good two miles to get educated. I wrapped my scarf around my mouth and nose to ward off the bitter cold and biting wind, but the scarf froze to my moist, warm mouth. Once we arrived at school, our first task was to defrost our toes and noses by the wood stove. To this day, my nose is sensitive to the slightest hint of cold. But the tribulations of getting there never affected how much I loved going to school.

We attended classes six days a week with no lunch break. Food was not offered at school. When we came home around one o'clock, we were ravenous for the lunch provided.

# PART 3

## MAY 1947 - OCTOBER 1956
## SURVIVAL

### DEAFENING SILENCE HANGS IN THE AIR

My family had survived "Uncle Hitler"! It was time to rebuild our lives, just as it was time for Germany to rebuild the nation. The next six years brought changes to the country and to us.

It was May 1947, springtime in our refugee camp in Neustadt bei Coburg, Bavaria. Springtime is a time of renewal. I was cheered by the sun warming the Earth, budding flowers, and singing birds, but I couldn't help noticing an uncanny stillness. Despite the birds, it seemed very quiet.

How strange it was to live without constant rumblings of cannons, gunshots, and war planes overhead! The silence was deafening, and for a long time I had the eerie sensation that something was missing. After all, we had grown accustomed to the constant barrage of calamity for six long years.

Germany was trying to rebuild and establish order after having endured such chaos. One daunting task that presented itself was the impending dissolution of the refugee camps: What should and could be done with the refugees? Who should be in charge, the Americans or the Russians? We wouldn't wait long for an answer.

## OUR NEW HOME UNDER THE ROOF

The West German authorities assigned us to new living quarters that would become our home for the next six years, the 250 to 300 foot attic room of a three-story house. The landlord was given no choice but to comply with our moving in. Unfortunately, we still didn't have a bathroom and had to go down a flight of stairs to use the common chemical toilet with no running water. Depending on the weather and temperatures, the odors could be unbearable. Anytime we needed water, we had to get it from a faucet a flight of stairs below us and carry it back up.

My parents slept in the main room on a mattress of sorts, which was stowed away during the day in one of the storage rooms that ran along the sides of the attic. My brothers slept in the larger storage room on a twin mattress, and I slept on a mattress in the smaller storage room. My room was under the eave, so I could hardly stand upright. The main room had a tiny stove with two gas burners, which allowed us to boil water and cook food. Once a month, we filled a large tub to take baths, one child after the other using the same water. Our furniture consisted of a small table with two benches and an old wardrobe that contained *the entire family's clothing*. Looking back, it's amazing how little we got by with, a stark difference compared to the abundance we think we need nowadays.

The winters brought frigid temperatures inside that house, as our living quarters were not caulked or insulated, and it was not uncommon for me to wake up with frozen eyelashes and eyebrows and a scarf frozen stiff as a board by my breath. Whatever the weather, I kept a scarf over my face to protect me from mice that shared the space with us. To this day, I have to have my hands and feet covered while sleeping.

My side of the house was in the shade, so in the summer, my room was pleasant; but my brothers, who slept on the opposite side, suffered suffocating heat as the sun beat down on the roof.

We would spend six years under these conditions—in my opinion, worse than the concentration camps we had endured. Our family wouldn't know the feeling of having our own place to call home until I was age sixteen.

## THE MARK LOSES VALUE AND PRICES RISE

My father was promoted by Siemens, where he worked as a bookkeeper, which allowed him to retire in 1977 with a good pension and benefits. Immediately following the war, we were able to survive on his income, but the help we continued to receive from our relatives in Detroit made all the difference to our well-being. If it had not been for them, we would have suffered as we had during the war years, like many others did.

I was only twelve years old, but I realized that prices were skyrocketing. Inflation was out of control; a loaf of bread cost one hundred marks, whereas it had been only one mark before the inflation. Currency reform took place in June 1948, bringing some relief. Store windows were filled with a bounty of food and goods again, but money was still scarce. Our neighbors continued to suffer hunger, and we shared whatever food we received from our relatives in America and from CARE.

## WOLLIN FAMILY GROWS

On March 15, 1950, my mother gave birth to my youngest brother, Martin. Since they had no access to an ambulance or to a car, my father accompanied my very pregnant mother on the half-hour walk to the only hospital in town.

These were hard times, and it was probably not wise to bring a child into the world, but no birth control was available.

My mother knew people would ridicule her for being poor and pregnant, so when she realized she was "in the family way," she tried to conceal her growing belly beneath large coats or under her *big, black handbag* until it was impossible to hide it any longer. Our family physician offered her an abortion because of the dire circumstances we lived in, but she refused his solution. Instead, she put herself in the Lord's hands, trusting His will only. I have to admire her for that. Throughout the rest of her life, she would be rewarded by the gift of my youngest brother, Martin.

In spite of our poverty, I was thrilled with the prospect of a new baby. I wanted a little sister, so I picked the name Andrea. But I allowed for another brother and chose the name Martin, after Dr. Martin Luther, the great reformer. It was as if I were prophesying that my little brother would someday do great things for the Lord, which, as a matter of fact, he did! But that is a story for another time.

## BEDBUGS AGAIN

We shared what we had with our landlord and neighbors, even though they looked down on us because we were refugees. Not once in the six years we lived there did our landlord or his wife allow us to set foot into their living quarters on the second floor. They accused us of bringing bedbugs into their house; my mother swore the bedbugs were already there when we moved in. Every night, until the house was fumigated, she picked the bedbugs off me while I tried to sleep, and dropped them in a bowl of water. My skin was very sensitive, and I suffered from lots of bites and boils.

When my little brother, Martin, was about four months old and asleep in the baby carriage, a bedbug bit him, and the doctor had to lance his tiny little finger. Once again, the little ones suffered.

## MISTAKEN IDENTITY

The mind plays strange tricks, provoking the following memory mingling birth and death. Martin's birth was my demise, or so it seemed. On the day after he was born, a tragic event occurred. My mother was still in the hospital, and two dear school friends of mine, Iris and Ingrid, pedaled their bicycles to visit another school friend, Walter. On their way home, Iris was struck by a car and killed instantly. She was the only child of a war widow. Somehow, my father was notified that *I* had been killed, and he went to identify the body. When he saw the boots sticking out from under the cover, he knew the body beneath did not belong to his daughter! For some time, whenever I thought of the mistaken identity, I had an eerie feeling, and it didn't help when people looked at me in surprise and said, "Is that really you? I thought you were dead!"

That eerie feeling came back later when I was again mistaken for dead. It happened about seven years later in the United States when a friend was killed in a car wreck, and I was presumed to be the one who had died. Then, in 1984 I almost lost my life in a car wreck. It took me six months to recuperate. At first, I thought Satan was trying to kill me, and it wasn't working. Then I understood it was the Lord telling me that when my time comes, it will be His doing, and there will be no question of mistaken identity, for He alone is in charge of my life.

Despite the strange occurrences after his birth, I loved my littlest brother passionately. He was the only one I shed tears over when I left Germany six years later. I still remember being at the train station, saying goodbye. Martin jumped into my arms and put his little legs around my waist, and we clung to each other for a few moments, weeping.

I often sang with him when he was supposed to take a nap and started crying. I taught him lots of songs. By the time he was two, he already knew more than a dozen. He was always musically gifted.

## MORE ABOUT SCHOOL

I enjoyed school, but I didn't fit in. It wasn't just the way I talked, but the way I looked, that made it difficult to blend in. I wore Salvation Army clothes sent from America, with funny-looking shoes, by German standards. Of course, I was thankful for the assistance, but I didn't feel comfortable.

However, school won over comfort. I started *Realschule*, the equivalent of high school, at age twelve and continued until

I was eighteen. Fourteen subjects were required, along with passing a test, before we could attend this level. Two foreign languages were mandatory, including English. I had six years of it, which was very good preparation for coming to the United States. For my second language, I chose Latin. Why would I choose a so-called dead language? Because I was dreaming of becoming a pediatrician, due to my love for children. Families had to pay for their children's books and school supplies, but my parents wanted all of us to get an education, so we did.

My favorite subjects were music, art, and religion, in which I always got As. Otherwise, my grades were so-so. When I got less than a B-minus, I was afraid to go home for fear of punishment. My mother knew we were capable of producing good grades and expected us to have no less than B-minuses. I hated chemistry and mathematics; history was boring, and physical education was not my cup of tea. I remember when I got C minuses on two tests and begged a friend of my mother's to come home with me, to keep her from punishing me. She obliged, but when she left, I got the whipping.

There were no proms or sports events at school, but I participated in concerts and plays, which I thoroughly enjoyed. These activities remain in my memory as highlights in an otherwise drab, poor life. My favorite school play was Shakespeare's *A Midsummer Night's Dream*. We performed on an outdoor stage against a mountain setting.

Besides school dramatics, churches and clubs put on plays for all seasons, and I participated in all of them. I played a dying girl in a Christmas play, and I was the princess in *The Princess and the Pea*. Besides reading, play acting was an escape for me in that dreary time.

## MY NUMBER ONE ESCAPE

My number one escape was reading because I could do it anywhere. I read by moonlight or with a flashlight under the covers. When I used a flashlight, my mother told me, "There's not enough light. Stop reading. You'll ruin your eyes!" However, when in recent years I did begin to lose my sight, it was from macular degeneration, a genetic disorder inherited from my father—*not from poor lighting*!

I preferred reading to eating. I frequently checked out books from the library. When I finished reading *Gone with the Wind* (in German, at that!), I cried for days because I didn't want it to end. My favorite books were novels about swashbuckling heroes rescuing damsels in distress. Of course, I always pictured myself as the distressed damsel.

## FRAU HOCH, THE PASTOR'S WIFE

Once we moved out of the camp into a real house, we started going to church regularly. I have warm memories of that time. We became acquainted with Pastor Hoch and his wife. She grew very fond of me and took me under her wing, perhaps because she didn't have children of her own.

At Christmastime, she took me and some of the other children to visit shut-ins and sing carols to them. I loved to sing. I wore an angel costume made of a light, summery fabric; I must have thought the angel persona would be enough to protect me from the windy, cold winter. As we walked from house to house, I shivered, and the pastor's wife draped her own fur coat around my shoulders. I loved going to church and to the youth group for girls, which *Frau* Hoch led.

Another Christmas, she decided that we kids should perform the nativity pageant for people living in little villages near Neustadt. Because there were no cars, one of the farmers allowed us to use his wagon and horse to get from place to place. We packed up the flat wagon with our props—a little manger, hay, and the baby Jesus doll—and dressed up in costumes for the play. I got to portray Mary, the mother of Jesus, and sing a solo at the manger. We traveled from village to village, spreading holiday joy. It was the most memorable, wonderful Advent that I can remember.

That was over sixty years ago, but I can still sing one of the songs: *Ich steh' an Deiner Krippe hier, O Jesu Du mein Leben.* "I stand here at the manger, O Jesus, my life. I come and bring to you everything you have given me, my spirit, soul and body. Take it and let it be pleasing to you."

When I sang those words at age twelve in the nativity play, I did not understand them. But I've learned that even when I don't understand, the Lord honors His word, especially when children sing to Him. When I left Germany, I chose another song to take with me to America, even though I didn't truly comprehend the words: *So nimm denn meine Haende* means "Take my hands now." The song continues: "and lead me, guide me, until the very end, because I cannot go alone, I cannot go without You, not even one step, wherever you are, there is where I want to be for all eternity."

My whole life has been a testimony to His faithfulness in fulfilling these words, even though I didn't know then what they fully meant.

## ESCAPE TO THE STAGE

I loved to read, I loved to sing, and I escaped my life through performing on stage. The little kids in our neighborhood gathered around me, wanting me to make a play, so I became their director. We rehearsed diligently and put on plays for five cents a ticket.

Frau Hoch's enthusiasm for children and the arts stayed with me. When I was a teenager, I led a youth group of twenty or thirty little girls. I took them on outings and helped them put on plays that delighted their parents.

We entertained ourselves in those days. We made our own fun because we had no movies, radio, or television. We didn't even have telephones, and texting and selfies weren't even specks in the future!

## INNOVATORS AND FRIENDS

Recently, my brother Lothar called me on the telephone from Germany. We got to reminiscing, and he reminded me how we used to make our own phone by fastening long strings from one empty can to another. We'd each take a can and run across the street, stop, face each other, and yell messages into the cans. As long as we stood in a straight line, the sound carried, but we couldn't hear each other around corners. We fixed that by yelling louder until we could hear each other. We had to laugh when we thought about it. We had fun, my brothers and I, and we hardly ever fought or even disagreed. We were good friends.

## PARENT TRAPS

My relationship with my parents was not so harmonious. I know that the Lord allowed love to come my way from people like Frau Hoch because I felt no love coming from my parents. My father was not a part of my everyday life because he worked, then played chess at his chess club whenever he could. He wasn't there when I needed him. When he was home, my parents argued a lot, mostly about the lack of money.

Ironically, it also seemed that Father often tried to buy Mother's love, letting her spend our resources foolishly.

One instance stands out in my memory:

My aunt in Detroit sent $400 for my mother to buy a sewing machine. She knew Mother was an expert seamstress and could sew clothes for the family, plus make extra money sewing for others. But my mother spent all the money on a real fur coat and accessories.

I can still see it: a black sable fur coat with alligator shoes and matching purse. Though they argued over finances a lot, my father didn't object to this, saying she looked beautiful. Meanwhile, we kids wore hand-me-downs. We didn't complain; we knew it wouldn't do any good.

Sometimes my father and mother were unanimous in their judgment against me. I'm thinking of the time I visited my friend Helga to celebrate her Confirmation. Confirmation was a big deal in Germany; it occurred when a young person turned fourteen and was confirmed in the Lutheran Church. Helga's mother, grandmother, and I were the only guests at her celebration, because Helga's father had died during the war, and she had no other family. My parents knew all this. It was a lively celebration with laughter and fancy cake and tea, and it lasted into the night. Helga's apartment was a few blocks from our house, and I was prepared to walk home.

About midnight the doorbell rang. Helga's mother opened the door and called to me. When I came to the door, I was surprised to see my father standing there with a coat pulled hastily over his pajamas. When he saw me, he reached out and slapped my face, hitting me so hard a tooth came loose. I knew my mother had pushed him to it. Years later my father apologized profusely, but at the time I was mortified and deeply hurt.

My mother's outbursts frightened me. I knew she'd had a strict upbringing, but that wasn't enough to make me understand her behavior. After all, I was a teenager with raging hormones, confused and frustrated, exploring, searching for the path to the rest of my life. My mother kept putting up roadblocks. She wouldn't let me participate in any activity with other teens unless it was school related. She kept saying, "What would other people think?" At other times, when I would tell her, "Everyone else is allowed to do this," she would say, "What other people do is none of our business." Very confusing to a young mind!

I don't know what my father thought, but he stayed out of it until the night of Helga's celebration.

I didn't know what to do, so I kept quiet and started dreaming about my escape to a better life.

## RELIGION IN HARD TIMES

My mother was a believer, though she sometimes failed miserably at her Christian walk. If she had ever shared her faith with me, I might have asked her why she did some of the things she did. But she never did share her beliefs with us children.

I was a keen observer, however, and I learned about religion and people who called themselves "religious." I learned that they did not always live up to their creed. Our landlady was one of those. As I said before, our family was assigned to the house she and her family owned; we got the third floor under the roof, and they had the second floor. She never invited us to visit. This woman was what I would call "holier than thou," because she claimed to be a good Christian but was snooty to us. She treated us like dirt because we had lost everything during the war.

They conducted religious meetings, and we were expected to attend. The meetings were held in an adjoining building, and they were boring. You'd think someone who preaches about the Lord would be full of love, but this woman was loveless, and she spread a loveless gospel. I could relate numerous examples of this behavior on her part, but will just say that much later, when I began to see the light and learned I Corinthians, Chapter 13, I found words that described that woman: "If you speak with the tongues of men and of angels and have not charity, you are like a sounding brass or tinkling cymbal." *Frau* Holier-than-Thou was full of sound and fury! I promised myself to have charity, even before I came to know the Lord for myself.

Of course, there were some truly religious people with love in their hearts, including a humble Sunday school teacher at the Lutheran church. She was an older spinster who often took my brothers and me home after church to feed us. She introduced us to potato dumplings, and she lived in a nice apartment. What a treat! I hope to thank her again someday, in heaven.

Pastor Hoch and his wife treated our family to delicious meals, including the pastor's special beer. I've already mentioned the kindness of his wife. He also taught religion classes in school, and I'll never forget his description of God and Jesus. The pastor drew a large circle on the blackboard. It looked like a big wheel. Then he drew many spokes connected to the middle hub. He explained that God was at the center, and the spokes were many religious ways to show us how to get to Him. Jesus was one of the spokes.

It took another fifteen years for me to sort this out in my own mind and heart. According to John 15:4, Jesus says, *"Ich bin der Weg, die Wahrheit und das Leben."* That means: "**I am** the way, **I am** the truth, **I am** the life, and no one comes to the Father but by Me." Jesus does not just SHOW us the way… He IS the way!

My greatest regret used to be that no one, not even my born-again mother, ever told me I needed to have a personal relationship with the Lord Jesus. I loved all the stories about Him in the Bible, and I am grateful I was raised where Scripture was taught in church and school. Without this foundation, it is easy to be led astray, and it can take a long time to find the way back. When I finally told the Lord I needed Him, it was because my life was in shambles. When I reread the diary I had started at age seventeen, I realize I had anticipated His plan. I wrote, "There's more to the Christian life, but I'm not ready. I first want to live, experience, and enjoy the pleasures of earthly life." And guess what! The Lord granted my request and let me make my own choices, with too many being wrong ones. Live and learn!

Many people have asked me to write about my personal conversion, and how I met the Lord. That is a story of another time, which I look forward to sharing.

## DREAMING OF ESCAPING POVERTY AND PARENTS

So, while I was wrestling with my hormones and my emotionally distant parents, I dreamed of escaping poverty, living on my own, owning a house, a car, a washing machine, and catching a good-looking husband. I knew all of this would never happen in Germany, and to make my dream come true, I would have to emigrate to the United States, with or without my family. This stubborn determination I inherited from my mother, who for better or worse, made a lifelong impression on me.

## MEANWHILE, LIFE GOES ON

One day my brothers and I came home from school to find an old piano squeezed into the main room on the third floor of the apartment house. My mother insisted we three needed it in order to take piano lessons from our former grade school teacher, *Frau*lein Aue. And so we did. I still have the Christmas songbook she gave me over sixty years ago.

Only a short time into the lessons I discovered that Lothar was the gifted one. One day, as I was coming up the stairs, I heard someone playing a familiar tune. When I entered the main room, I saw Lothar sitting at the piano playing without sheet music. It was a song we had not learned during our lessons. I was impressed. I knew I could never do that, and after a year, I quit. I wish to this day that the Lord had seen fit to give me some of Lothar's talent, which He also bestowed, in abundance, on Martin.

I couldn't play piano, but I loved to sing. I have a feeling that, if I had concentrated and pursued my love for acting, singing, and dancing, I might have achieved something in these areas. Years later, I found out that all of my cousins assumed, when they found out we were emigrating to California, that I would want to become a Hollywood star. They were sure I would have a career in acting, but I never thought I was pretty enough or had "what it takes."

Anyway, my aspirations did not yearn for a singing or acting career. What I wanted was to establish a loving home and have children—lots of them, if I had enough money. My parents never encouraged me in any direction; my mother's strict Baptist background prohibited her from encouragement, and my father did not care one way or another. I'm glad the Lord was looking out for me, and I'm thankful He kept me from going to Hollywood.

## REMEMBERING SWEET MOMENTS

Though I aspired to motherhood and lots of children, I struggled with my own mother and her less than empathetic relationship to me. Sometimes, however, especially at Advent and Christmas, our home was very happy. We always celebrated with candles and music, as most people do in Germany. The season was extra special for us because, on Christmas Eve, my mother was always nice, and that meant more to me than any gift.

Not that we received lots of presents. We usually got only one present each (one year I got none), and a *bunten Teller,* a colorful plate filled with candy, cookies, and **an orange**. I gave my share of the candy to my brothers in exchange for their oranges, because they were a rare delicacy, and because I never liked chocolate. The peaceful atmosphere with my mother during Advent was very important to me. It almost made up for the other times when she was not so kind.

My mother did nice things for other people all the time, serving in church, working with the Red Cross, and volunteering, and she received lots of commendations and praise for taking charge and accomplishing good works. But she never turned her attention to me. She never asked how I was, how I felt, or what I needed. That omission created a void in my heart. In my diary, I swore that if I ever had children, I'd never put my family second to anyone.

Later in life, I understood and forgave her. I realized that she and my father were products of their upbringing and environment and couldn't help what they became because of what they had experienced. But when I was a teenager, my parents' attitude made it easier for me to leave them behind and seek a new life. When I had made that new life, and found the Lord, I forgave them.

As soon as my father retired from Siemens, my parents started coming to visit us in the United States every other year, staying four to eight weeks at a time, over the span of twenty years. I was happy to take good care of them during each vacation until their passing. I honored them, according to the Word.

## ALWAYS HUNGRY

During my teen years in the third-floor apartment, all of Germany was always hungry. The Bible says that we can make our bellies our God. When you're hungry, you believe in a full belly. Hunger can drive people to actions they wouldn't ordinarily do—to lying, cheating, and stealing—just to survive. I sympathize with people in countries where lack of food has driven them to rioting and criminal acts. I have to thank the Lord that we, because of His mercy, were spared from such desperate measures to survive.

But the struggle for food did drive us to consume things we previously believed inedible, like horsemeat. We were told horsemeat was very lean and healthy, and I have to admit it didn't taste that bad. We learned to appreciate what food we had and not waste it. To this day, I won't allow the waste of food in my house.

When I was about twelve or thirteen, we invited a mother and her two children to our house for lunch. She was the wife of a US soldier, and we were so excited to see "Americans," we could hardly wait. My mother had saved our meat food stamps in order to serve pork chops to them. Just them, mind you, not us. To our utter horror, the woman's kids took two bites, pushed their plates away, and wanted something else. They whined and misbehaved until their mother took them away. Fortunately, my frugal mother had saved the picked-at chops, and we got to eat after all. This was my first lesson about Americans wasting food.

There was, however, one food product that stands out in my memory. We received a package from Detroit that included a can of Spam. We had never heard of Spam, but we took to it immediately. My brother Fred and I were recovering from the "mumps" and this was the first taste of food in days. I can still remember the delight in tasting it.

## MUTTI'S SUNDAY WALKING REGIMEN

After a good Sunday meal, my mother insisted we go out for exercise, and every Sunday we took walks. I didn't much like walking and would have preferred to read a book. I vowed that I would never make my children walk. My mother insisted we walk nice and slow, and we were not allowed to run ahead or play while walking. We children hated those walks!

But there were other walks we enjoyed, longer walks to the border. Neustadt bei Coburg was situated directly on the border between East and West Germany. We looked across barbed wire fences, minefields, ditches, and watchtowers to see German guards on the other side. Families in Neustadt had relatives on the other side, but they couldn't visit them. After some years and expensive visas, they were allowed occasional contact, but they had to take the train the long way around from the opposite direction. They were never able to walk the couple of miles across the border to be with their relatives. As a consequence of Germany's great sin, it would be thirty-five years before the wall in Berlin and the borders came down.

But when we lived in Neustadt, we loved walking to the border and talking to the American soldiers. My father was studying English, and he taught us a few phrases. We had fun chatting with the soldiers, and the soldiers always gave us gum and candy. When we talked with a nice young black soldier, we discovered he was from Detroit, where our relatives lived. We gave him my aunt's address and told him to visit her when he got back after his time in Germany was up. He promised he would, and he did. But we got in a lot of trouble with our relatives, and they asked that we never do that again. My aunt tried to explain that things were different in America. The fact that the soldier was black caused problems for our relatives!

To my utter horror, I found out she was right when I came to the United States in 1956. Except for the growing knowledge of Hitler's atrocities, this was my first experience with racial hatred and bigotry.

## LONELINESS AND LONGING

When I was very young, I felt I was different and didn't belong. It even occurred to me that I might be adopted. Of course, I wasn't! But I was lonely and longed for something I believed I could find by coming to the United States. Perhaps this persistent craving was to escape the stark, loveless land that had consumed me; my birthplace. Perhaps I never felt embraced by it or its people, even in all its splendor and beauty. Perhaps we were all still healing from the ravages of war.

I was not a conformist, and I hated following crowds. Local events that mattered to everyone else didn't mean a thing to me. When a movie was made in our town, everybody was excited but me. I was never a "hero worshipper" of mere humans.

One day, I was walking home from school when someone dumped a bucket of water on my head from a tall building. I didn't know who the perpetrator was until a couple of years later, when Helga, who was now my friend, told me she had done it. She said she didn't like the way I held my head so high.

I was "a stranger in a strange land," waiting for deliverance. As my loneliness and longing increased, my isolation spurred me to search for a better life across the ocean in America.

When my parents tried to emigrate to the United States, and were rejected because of my father's tuberculosis scars, it was clear we wouldn't be going as a family. I didn't yet know that the merciful hand of God was leading me when I decided to pursue my future plans alone.

## SNAPSHOTS OF MY TEENAGE YEARS IN NEUSTADT

Apart from the *Sturm und Drang* playing out in my mind, the storm and stress of my teenage years played out in Neustadt one way and another.

As I have said, my hormones were in a state of flux, as I became aware of the opposite sex, and there was no one to talk to because there was no talking about sex at home or school, and most certainly not in church. All I knew from my mother was that men were bad, looking for one thing to be avoided like the plague. I was told that if I ever "did anything," I would be disowned. At sixteen, I was so naive that when a boy gave me a French kiss in a dark hallway on my birthday, I worried that I was pregnant.

Until I was seventeen, I was a real tomboy. I loved to run and play, preferably with boys because I had three brothers and

I was used to roughhousing with them. Swimming, climbing trees, and beating boys at everything was great fun. Once I beat every boy in my class by wrestling each one to the ground until he cried "Uncle!"

My brother Lothar and I were always up to something, but it was always poor Lothar who managed to hurt himself. We were picking wild blueberries in the nearby mountain forest. It was safe in those days for kids to ramble off in the woods, even as far as an hour's walk from home. When it was close to dusk, we started back. We came to a hill, challenged each other to a race, and ran down. Lothar got his feet tangled, fell into barbed wire, and tore open his upper left thigh. That was scary! He was crying and bleeding. We got him up, helped him walk to town to find the nurse's house, and she took us all to the doctor. There were no telephones in those days, so by the time we got home, it was dark. We knew we were in trouble and expected to be punished, but we were spared when our parents learned what had happened.

As I've said before, I was unusually attached to my mother. I idolized her but was never able to please her. When I was about sixteen, she went to visit relatives in Hamburg and was gone for over two weeks. She took little Martin and left me in charge of my brothers as well as my father, whom we hardly ever saw. When she returned, I was excited to show off my housekeeping skills. I had cleaned our little apartment, cooked dinner, and put a vase of wildflowers on the table. I was sure she'd be pleased and couldn't wait for her praise. It never came. Instead, she looked under the wardrobe, discovered dust bunnies, and scolded me. I just couldn't get it right.

Another time I decided, all on my own, to do the dishes. This was quite a procedure that entailed fetching water and heating it. My mother was writing a letter to her relatives in Detroit when I told her what I had done and how good I felt, having washed the dishes without being asked. She didn't even look up. She told me to leave her alone; she wasn't interested to hear what I'd done as long as it was done.

I've long since forgiven her, but I haven't forgotten, because it hurt deeply. I made a mental note to pay attention to my kids. I hope they have always known how much I appreciate their efforts.

Another time my mother told me that if I scrubbed all the stairs in the apartment house we lived in, I might get fifty cents to join the neighbor kids in a planned activity. I agreed, even though the house had three stories with a lot of stairs. When I finished the job, she informed me I wasn't allowed to participate after all, nor did I get the fifty cents. I was crushed; I had worked hard, and I really wanted to go with my friends.

This is probably why I made it a point to take my kids out of school if necessary, to go on trips, to write notes so they could go skiing on school days, to give them an abundance of experiences.

When I was a child, we attended the Lutheran Church, and I loved it. The church was beautiful. I can shut my eyes and see the huge, beautiful stained-glass window behind the altar where Martin Luther preached five hundred years before. I can read the stained-glass window in my mind's eye: "In the beginning was the Word and the Word was with God." (John 1:1) As I sat in church, I studied and memorized every detail of that beautiful window.

Once, during Advent, Lothar and I and some other kids went to midweek service. We sat in the second balcony facing the altar below. An old preacher, whom none of us liked, was in the pulpit. In church school, he would hit us over the heads with the Bible if we didn't know our lessons. So here he was, standing below us, swaying from one side to the other, droning on and on. In my line of vision was a hanging chandelier. I watched the old preacher sway back and forth on either side of the big light fixture. I tried to stifle a giggle as I nudged my brother and friends. They got a kick out of it, too, and then we all started laughing. Over and over we tried to quit but just couldn't. We thought to stifle our mirth by hunkering down in our seats; just as the old preacher looked up, we ran.

That was when my mother began to call me a "nail in her coffin."

But when it came to my faith, I was high-spirited and ready to defend my convictions. On one of our field trips I got into a fistfight with my friend, Gisela, who was Catholic. We rolled on the grass in a meadow, arguing over Mary, the mother of Jesus. As much as I loved portraying Mary in church plays, I knew she wasn't equal to Jesus or the Queen of Heaven. I tried to beat this truth into my friend's head.

The local newspaper wrote an article about our fight, and the relationship between the Lutheran and the Catholic youth got better. We learned to accept our differing views and work together. Gisela and I are friends to this day and have often laughed about our squabble.

During the six years we lived in that attic apartment, time stood still. A year seemed like an eternity, compared to the way time flies today. We lived a few minutes from the train station, and my heart ached whenever I saw a train leaving. I wanted to be on it. I had *Fernweh*, the opposite of "homesickness." The English word *wanderlust* means a desire to travel, and that comes close, but *Fernweh* is more than a desire; it is a need. I *needed* to travel. I believed happiness and fulfillment waited for me away from poverty, my parents, and everyone and everything I had ever known.

## A NEW APARTMENT

In June 1953, my family was assigned a new apartment outside of town. Siemens had built several three-story apartment houses for employees, and we were allowed to rent one because my father worked for the company. Our apartment was approximately nine hundred square feet. Once again it was on the third floor under a roof with slanting walls, but we were thrilled because it had **a bathroom with a flush toilet and a bathtub**. The apartment had a tiny kitchen with running water and a gas stove, and two tiny bedrooms, one for my parents and one for my brothers. I slept on the couch in the small living room for three years. But because we finally had **our own bathroom**, I didn't mind.

# LOOKING BACK

Looking back on my life in Germany, I have to say the years between 1953 and 1956 were the most difficult. Despite the trauma, danger, deprivation, hunger, and persecution of the war years, my teenage years were at times so unbearable, I contemplated suicide. I considered walking into a lake to drown myself, but I was an excellent swimmer, and I knew that wouldn't work.

I know now that I played with all those thoughts out of self-pity, encouraged by the Devil. I'm glad I didn't succumb to Satan and kept hoping for a better life in the United States.

# MY FIRST REAL JOB

In 1953, thanks to the help the United States had given Germany, the economy improved rapidly. During high school, I had several odd jobs and made enough money to buy a bicycle. After a year of college, I quit school to take a job in Siemens' bookkeeping department. I'm convinced this was a result of God's foresight, because that job helped me more than any of my schooling when I came to the United States to find employment.

Maybe because we lived in dire poverty for so many years, the Lord gave me a heart to be mindful of others. Out of my first paycheck, I gave half to charities. To this day, I continue to share with those who have not been blessed with the abundance I have received.

But not everyone was charitable. I resented having to give a goodly amount of every meager paycheck to my mother for my keep, especially when I realized other mothers helped their families by working outside the home or taking in work at home. Our little town of Neustadt was known as the "Doll Town of Bavaria," because dolls and toys were produced there and shipped throughout the world. So, there were lots of jobs for people who knew how to sew. My mother, an excellent seamstress, never worked outside or inside our home, even though she did not hesitate to enjoy the advantages of money.

One day I was called away from my job at Siemens for an emergency at home. I pedaled hard a good half hour, arriving to find leftovers from a delicious breakfast, and real coffee from America, still on the table and my mother in bed complaining of heart trouble. I think she actually had indigestion. She often claimed to have heart trouble, but it never materialized until she passed away at age eighty.

I learned from my mother, and I made mental notes on how *not* to raise my children. Later in America, I decided not to spend money on fancy lunches when I had three beautiful children and worked full-time as a single mom to support them. Only once a week did I allow myself $2.98 for a patty melt. Back then, that amount paid for gas to take the kids and their friends to the coast on the weekend. Doing without was worth it.

## TEENAGE ANGST

I always loved to dance, and I begged my father over and over to let me take ballroom dance lessons with all the other kids. My mother, as a good Baptist, could not give her consent. But finally, my father relented.

Two brothers in our town were developmentally disabled, and I felt sorry for them because of the ridicule they endured. To make them feel better, I let them take me, one at a time, to the ball, which always took place at the end of the dance lessons. I didn't give it another thought, but many years later when I visited Germany, I learned they had never forgotten and how much they had appreciated my gesture.

All Germans like their beer and wine, even strict Baptists! My mother would make her own blueberry wine, and Fred and I would go down to the cellar and slurp a few sips right out of the crock, ready or not. Then we would go out together to dance, sometimes pretending we were boyfriend and girlfriend. We both loved dancing but got in trouble if our parents found out. When they did, it devastated me to be scolded, grounded, and punished. But Fred just laughed and did it again as soon as he could.

During the times we wined and danced, I observed that many people only had a good time when they had a lot to drink. I didn't like the way people looked and acted when they drank too much. That's when I decided that I could have a great time and even be the belle of the ball without drinking at all. I didn't have to decide whether or not to use drugs because, in those days, drugs were unheard of. I tried smoking cigarettes once and almost choked to death; I got violently sick to my stomach. I never tried to inhale again, until many years later in the United States.

I was a late bloomer. At seventeen I had not had a period and I was as flat as a board, but I was interested in boys as more than playmates. I couldn't understand why the other girls had steady boyfriends. Worrying about it made me lonely and unhappy.

Eventually I bloomed, and I even had a few serious proposals. While I was yearning to go to the United States, I met a young man at a party who wanted to get engaged and follow me to America. But my heart was not touched by his offer. I knew better things awaited me out there on the other side of the world.

Shortly before I left for America, there was an incident that could have changed my life. I was at a youth gathering in the mountains, led by a new, young pastor who had recently moved to town with his beautiful young wife. After one of our singing sessions around the campfire, he took me aside and told me he loved me. He said he would divorce his wife and marry me if I would just stay in Germany. If this had happened sooner, when I wished for a boyfriend and before I'd filled out the papers to emigrate, who knows what I might have done? As it was, I gave him a lecture on fidelity, the Word of God, and honor in general. The young pastor insisted he would never forget me or stop loving me. A few weeks later I left Germany and never saw him again. I heard he left our town not many years later, for better places.

One of my greatest acts of rebellion was cutting my hair, something I had been forbidden to do all my life. When I was earning my own money at age eighteen, I went to a salon, had my hair cut, and even got a permanent. My mother was furious; she would have thrown me out had there been somewhere for me to go. But my rebellion made up for the tears I had shed when all my girlfriends came to school with their hair cut shoulder length and mine was still wound around my head in braids. I was never allowed to wear my hair open and long, except in school plays when I was acting a role.

In another act of rebellion, when I was about seventeen, I put on lipstick after leaving the house and the glare of my mother's eyes. She forbade lipstick because she didn't want a "floozy" for a daughter. My mother condemned any attempts I made to look attractive or fashionable, saying they were vanity. I expect that's why I allowed my own daughter total freedom of choice in her teenage years.

## PREPARING TO LEAVE GERMANY

For over two years I tried to get permission from the American Immigration Department to emigrate to the United States. Finally, when I turned eighteen, I could apply for a visa by myself.

My brother Fred was nineteen and decided to do the same. Mountains of paperwork followed, the vetting extremely extensive, and we had to go to Munich to pass tests. At that time, everyone who wanted to emigrate had to pass mental, physical, psychological, and criminal tests in order to get a visa. Criminal records wouldn't even allow minor offenses like traffic tickets. Of course, there was no danger there since we never owned a car. I have often wondered if everyone would benefit if at least some of this policy were applied today.

Fred and I also had to get a sponsor in America. This was handled through the World Council of Churches.

We did get to choose what state we wanted to go to, and Fred and I chose California for two reasons: beautiful pictures and glowing reports about the prosperity of the state. Plus, it was a long way away from Detroit and our mother's Baptist relatives! While our family was spared from starvation through their generosity, I could never accept how they had treated the American soldier who had showed up on their doorstep. Seeing the American soldiers, the scent of their colognes and the sight of them chewing gum was one of the few highlights of an otherwise lonely childhood, and teenage girl. My admiration for American soldiers swelled during postwar years in Germany, solidifying my eagerness to come to America.

Fred picked the town of Tulare, California, because Bob Mathias, the Gold Medal Olympian, was born there. In 1974, I met Bob Mathias in Washington, D.C., when I was representing Cal Bean & Grain, the farmers' cooperative I worked for.

## IMAGES FROM GERMANY

I couldn't wait to leave Germany, and I knew I was not going to miss it. However, in the vault of my memory, two lovely images are preserved, one from our apartment and one from the train the day Fred and I left our native country. I reflect on these mental pictures sometimes.

My favorite memory of our apartment is a view from the living room, overlooking quaint buildings and my beloved church. It is a winter night close to Christmas. Snow is falling, blanketing the town, beautiful and still. *Stille Nacht.* I gaze out the window taking it in. All at once church bells peal, and their sound drifts, long and melodious over the snow. When the bells stop, a choir of trumpets begins, playing a beautiful Advent hymn about the coming of the King: *Macht hoch die Tuer, die Tor macht weit* ("Lift up the gates, the King is coming"). It is a sign of hope.

The second image is a collage of changing scenes on the train to Hamburg in 1956. Fred and I travel through a gorgeous valley, lush with trees, ripe with wheat fields, and dazzling with late-blooming wildflowers under a blue sky with cumulus clouds. It is a sign of peace and prosperity.

These images are like postcards from the Lord, sent to remind me that the Germany I grew up in wasn't all bad.

## LEAVING GERMANY

In mid-September 1956, Fred and I planned to spend a week with our relatives in Hamburg before leaving for America. But Fred got sick with the flu and debated whether to cancel his decision to leave with me for the United States. I couldn't believe it! I had my heart set on leaving, and I wanted him with me.

Then I pulled myself together and mentally put a rod of iron down my back. I swallowed hard and told him it was okay, I'd go by myself. I know I would have. Nothing could have made me stay. Fortunately, Fred rallied and was well enough to go with me.

The day we left, we said goodbye to our parents and young Lothar and Martin at the train station, and the only crying I did was when I held my brother Martin. I knew I might never see my family again, but I couldn't wait for the train to pull out of the station.

## GRATEFUL FOR MY GERMAN YEARS

Over the years, I have learned to appreciate many experiences of my growing up in Germany. I appreciate the education I received, both secular and religious, even though it was not always pleasant. Because of the lack of funds for other recreation, I learned to love the arts and reading, which is still my favorite pastime. I also loved nature, and Germany's natural beauty could never be destroyed by the evil of Hitler's war.

Strange as it may seem, I am even thankful for a strict mother. I was a strong-willed child, and there is no telling what would have happened to me had she not kept such a tight rein on me.

Looking back over the terrible years of war and postwar experiences, I would not change a single thing. When the Lord Jesus became real to me, at age thirty, the craving for human love and support faded, and I could accept my past and pack it away in a *big, black handbag* to share with others on occasion.

My only regret is that it took me so long to discover that only in Him would I receive peace and contentment.

## GERMANY WAS WRONG

Before I leave the shores of Germany, I need to add something. Even though I was a little girl during the war and a teenager thereafter, I understood, from the news and from our own devastated lives, that Germany deserved the judgment of God. From then until now, I never held any of the bombings or terrible conditions we experienced against any country that saw the necessity of bringing Germany to its knees, whatever the cost, even to the innocent children.

Another thing I want to acknowledge: if it hadn't been for the generosity and the caring of the United States when Germany was in ruins, many would not have survived after the war. Through the Marshall Plan and the other caring organizations, the United States helped West Germany to recover and become a thriving, healthy nation again. The consequences and aftermath of the Holocaust will never totally be erased or healed until Jesus comes. I believe that, as a German, it is my duty and privilege to keep alive the memory of this great evil that my country committed against the "Apple of His Eye," the Jews. My commitment to pray for the peace of Jerusalem and to help financially, as the Lord directs, will not waver until I die or He comes to bring justice and equity to all. I have been a supporter of The Chosen Peoples Ministry for over forty years.

## ALL ABOARD, AT LAST!

Finally, the day came—September 25, 1956! Fred and I and our suitcase were loaded on a worn-out army freighter in Hamburg. The other passengers, approximately two thousand, included mainly young single people from throughout Western Europe. Only a few had escaped from the East, and I think every country was represented. Later, we learned that the freighter was overloaded by two hundred to three hundred people. No one wanted to be left behind, so we made do.

# CROSSING THE OCEAN

Single women and girls were assigned to one deck and single men and boys to another. The few families had separate cabins. Each deck had community bathrooms and showers, and there was one big mess hall where meals were taken in shifts. It was all very exciting. Even with the babble of so many different languages, we young people had fun communicating the best we could. I even had two or three marriage proposals! Of course, I declined them, knowing how much better I could do with an American, instead of one of these penniless boys from Europe. One of the young men I met on the ship found me about two years later, in California, and proposed again. But I was married and had my first son, so I kindly sent him away.

Shortly into the ten-day voyage, there was a storm, and a scourge of seasickness broke out on the ship, lasting more than four days. I was so sick I thought that if I could just die, I would be happy. Seasickness is a terrible affliction! The ship personnel told us the worst thing to do was give up and lie down on our bunks. They told us to eat, even if it came right up again, and to go up on deck for fresh air. After two days of wanting to die, I did what I was told and it worked, even though I had to hang over the rail and feed quite a few fish for a while.

As I recuperated, a young mother with three children was assigned to my care; I was to help them get well. In the meantime, I couldn't find Fred anywhere, until I took the liberty of going to the men's deck. When I stepped into his quarters, I almost got sick again because the stench was so overwhelming. I pulled my brother from his bunk and hauled him up on deck, where I put him on the floor under a tarp, safe from the howling wind. I made him eat, and after a couple of days, he got well. I have not been on a big ship since. Sometimes I think I'd like to take a cruise and then I think, *Maybe not!*

## GREETED BY A BEAUTIFUL LADY

The sight of the Statue of Liberty and the New York skyline will be with me until time is no more. It was October 4, 1956, and we were finally in the land of promise, the melting pot of all nations, the place of justice and opportunity for all. So we were told. We took our place with the overwhelming crowds in the harbor house, where it took hours and hours of waiting to hear our names called, to be debriefed and registered. Finally, we had our green cards and instructions to get to California. The authorities gave us five dollars each and loaded us, with our one suitcase, on the train to California.

## CALIFORNIA, HERE I COME!

None of the people on our freighter was on the train with us, but we quickly found other Germans traveling west. It took three days to get to California. There were no sleepers on the train, and we were given one pillow. There was a bathroom with no shower. I'm sure some deodorant would have been appreciated by our fellow travelers, but we had experienced deprivation during the war, and this was no big deal for us.

We were very hungry so we decided to buy a cheese sandwich. The first shock was that it cost a whole dollar! The second and bigger shock was our first experience with American "rainbow bread," two cotton-like pieces with nothing to chew and a thin slice of American cheese between, leaving us as hungry as before. Unbeknownst to us, a nice young man had observed our encounter with the cheese sandwich. I guess he felt sorry for us and bought us our first hamburger at the next station. I knew Hamburg was a city in Germany, but I had never heard of hamburgers.

What I remember most from those three days on the train is how unbelievably tired I was. I yearned for enough space to lie down and sleep, but I had to sit up the whole time. At some point, I must have drifted off, because the next thing I knew, it was a new day and I opened my eyes to California!

# Deep Gratitude
— a prayer by Mother Theresa

*"Help me speak your fragrance wherever I go. Flood my soul with your spirit and life. Penetrate and possess my whole being so utterly that my life may only be a radiance of yours. Shine through me and be so in me that every soul I come in contact with may feel your presence in my soul. Let them look up and see no longer me but only Jesus! Stay with me and then I will begin to shine as you shine, so to shine as to be a light to others. The light, oh Jesus, will be all from you. None of it will be mine. It will be you shining on others through me. Let me thus praise you in the way that you love best, by shining on those around me. Let me preach you without preaching, not by words but by example, by the catching force, the sympathetic influence of what I do, the evident fullness of the love my heart bears for you. Amen."*

# AFTERWORD

All my life, reading has been my passion and escape from loneliness. I agree with C. S. Lewis, one of my favorite writers, who wrote, "We read to know we're not alone." I like writers who provide conclusions in books that have no definitive endings.

So here is my epilogue: What I most want my story to convey is that the Lord led me through the trials and tribulations of my life so that I could find meaning, joy, and peace. Because I am approaching the end of my life, I want to inspire my readers to question their own choices, priorities, and values in order to find peace with the Lord and joy in their hearts.

My life in America has been full of challenges, with treks over mountaintops and through valleys, sometimes of despair. Many decisions caused by wrong choices proved to be learning experiences, but through it all, I saw the hand of God, His faithfulness and Mercy. He can be there for my readers as well.

When I give talks about my life in Germany, I am often asked to come back to tell "the rest of my story" in America. One time, however, I was told by representatives of a Christian organization that I would not be able to tell the rest of the story because I had been divorced. In the end, those representatives backed down because too many people requested to hear my story, warts and all.

I have accepted my life, and I am not ashamed because the Lord has accepted me.

I am eternally grateful that we are accepted in the Beloved just as we are by our Father in heaven, as it says in Ephesians 1:6. Lest anyone think I wish the suffering during my life would not have happened, I can honestly say I don't. God's Word explains it best: "Through it all, the Lord has completely delivered me from the fear of death, because we are truly held in bondage by that fear all the days of our lives." (Hebrews 2:15)

The choices we make to fill the void this fear creates are the roots of all the suffering we experience, but He is able to deliver us, if we let Him! To be set free from fear is a gift that can come through suffering. I have no regrets, except where my bad choices have hurt others, and for that I turn to the fathomless forgiveness of our Lord.

"One of the greatest blessings that comes through our own suffering is the ability to truly feel with others in their suffering and be of comfort to them." (2 Corinthians 1:3 and 4) If we've walked in their shoes, as the saying goes, our sympathy will come from the heart.

My heart breaks every time I see the tremendous suffering of little ones all over this planet. It makes me want to live to give, to do my part to alleviate some of it. But the promise in the Scriptures is that the day will come when there shall be war no more, and God Himself will wipe away all tears; there shall be no more death, neither sorrow nor crying, and neither shall there be any more pain. Above all, there will be no more sin!

I have two favorite sayings, always applicable in any situation: "This too shall pass" and "The best is yet to come." It is a matter of having faith.

I could fill countless pages with arguments for the Lord's beneficence, but I will leave it here: Many of my illusions, dreams, aspirations, and desires are gone or changed, thank God, and only one remains—to be of help to all those whom He has brought my way, and to know, love, and serve Jesus, for He is truly worthy!

Philippians 2:5-11 says, "Let this mind be in you, which was also in Christ Jesus, Who thought it not robbery to be equal with God, but made Himself of no reputation. He took on the form of a servant and was made in the likeness of men. And being found in the fashion of a man He humbled Himself and became obedient unto death, even the death of the Cross. Wherefore God has also highly exalted Him and given Him a name that is above all names, that at the name of Jesus every knee will bow, of things in heaven and things on earth and under the earth, and every tongue will confess that Jesus Christ is Lord, to the Glory of God the Father!"

Finally, I want to close with my favorite prayer from the Word of God in Ephesians 3:14-21: "For this cause I bow my knees to the Father of our Lord Jesus Christ, by Whom the whole family in heaven and earth is named, that He may grant you, according to the riches of His glory, to be strengthened with might by His Spirit in the inner man, that Christ may dwell in your hearts by faith, and you being rooted and grounded in love, will be able to comprehend, with all saints, what is the breath and length and depth and heights, and to know the love of Christ, which passes knowledge, that you might be filled with all the fullness of God. Now unto Him Who is able to do exceeding, abundantly above all that we could ask or think, according to the power which works in us, unto Him be glory in the church, by Christ Jesus, throughout all ages, world without end. Amen."

# SUGGESTED READING

First and foremost, read and study the Bible. Ask the Spirit of Truth to show you Truth and He will, at all times. I use Strong's *Exhaustive Concordance* and Vine's *Expository Dictionary* for the original Greek definitions. You don't have to be a scholar to understand God's Word, I promise.

For those who are pressed for time, in His mercy we have been given the *One Year Bible* for anyone who desires to read through the whole Bible in a very easy, balanced program. It includes the Old Testament, Psalms, and Proverbs, plus the New Testament in daily portions for 365 days. In addition, the Bible is available on tape and CD. I have worn out several tapes listening to the New Testament. Faith comes by hearing, and hearing by the Word of God!

So, you see, there is no excuse for not knowing the Bible!

I also know that daily devotionals are of great value, showing the application of Scripture to daily life. I have some favorite devotionals that have spoken to me for many years on my journey. Oswald Chambers' *My Utmost for His Highest* would be number one. All of Chambers' writings are Christ-centered and full of truth, well worth reading and rereading. *Streams in the Desert* and *Springs in the Valley*, by Mrs. Charles Cowman, along with *Jesus Calling*, by Sarah Young, are also good soul food.

The classic devotional *God Calling*, by Two Listeners, includes the often-repeated admonition "Love and Laugh," which I practice as much as possible by keeping an eternal outlook. Worshipful, Christ-centered music (tune in to "familyradio.org" for 24/7 traditional Christian music) as part of our quiet time definitely softens our hearts and gives us ears to hear what the Holy Spirit has to teach us concerning Jesus.

All of Andrew Murray's books, plus everything C. H. Spurgeon and Basilea Schlink, founder of the Evang Sisterhood of Mary in Germany, are full of spiritual nourishment.

I just reread *Passion for Jesus*, by Mike Bickle. What a treasure! Another book worthy to read more than once is *The Signature of Jesus*, by Brennan Manning. If you want to know what goes on in other parts of the world right now, read the *Heavenly Man*, by Brother Yun. You'll find it unbelievable at times, but absolutely true and supported by secular news.

Add all the classics by Fenelon, Madam Guyon, Michael Molinos, Brother Andrew, Thomas a' Kempis, and many more, and your soul will truly be made fat, as it says in the Word.

These are just a few of what is all available at any time.

I do warn you, many of these suggested readings will challenge and maybe disturb you, but also inspire you to know Him better, our soon coming King, and to love Him more and serve Him with all your heart, forever and ever for He alone is worthy.

And guess what? With unbelievable humility He says, in Revelation 3:20, "Behold, I stand at the door and knock, if any one hears my voice and opens the door I will come into him and dine with him and he with Me."

One more thing: "Jesus loves you this I know, for the Bible tells me so!" I used to sing this song to my grandchildren while rocking them to sleep.

Happy reading, dear readers!

www.ingramcontent.com/pod-product-compliance
Lightning Source LLC
Chambersburg PA
CBHW071740080526
44588CB00013B/2102